NEBRASKA

The Missouri River has been the takeoff point for many events in Nebraska history. This nuclear-powered electrical generating plant at Fort Calhoun needs abundant water for cooling and thus uses the stream in still another historic role. The plant is operated by the Omaha Public Power District. A similar facility is operated by the Nebraska Public Power District at Brownville, also on the Missouri.

NEBRASKA
A Pictorial History

Bicentennial Edition (Revised and Enlarged)

Compiled by Bruce H. Nicoll
Revised by Gilbert M. Savery

UNIVERSITY OF NEBRASKA PRESS • LINCOLN

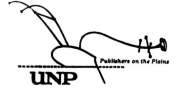

Library of Congress Cataloging in Publication Data
Nicoll, Bruce Hilton, 1912–
    Nebraska: a pictorial history.

    1. Nebraska—History—Pictorial works. I. Savery,
Gilbert M., 1917–   11. Title.
F667.N5 1975   978.2'0022'2   75–3570
ISBN 0–8032–0863–4
ISBN 0–8032–5825–9 Pbk

Foreword

In this chronicle of Nebraska, presented through extensive use of paintings, drawings, and photographs, I have attempted to show how four generations of Nebraskans have transformed a vast stretch of empty prairie into a state which has made significant contributions to—and received much from—a great nation.

The story of our state is at once one of optimism and doubt, promise and frustration, success and failure. The difficulty was that the Nebraska settler brought with him the tools and the political institutions of settlement which had worked well in the East but were found to be something less than satisfactory for the frontier country west of the Missouri River. Since most of our state lies within the limits of the Great Plains, we have been the inheritors of all the assets and liabilities of that region. It is a region which offers man more reasons for success and more causes for failure than any other geographical area of our nation. If, in Nebraska, there is a central fact of life, a common denominator of existence, it must be geography—weather, soil, water, and the lay of the land. It is its geography, for example, that has given Nebraska not one, but two faces. In the subhumid eastern sector the appearance and the point of view of the people are midwestern. Beyond the ninety-eighth meridian, Nebraskans take on a western look and outlook engendered by the big sky and broad horizon of the cattle country. It is literally true that Nebraska is where the Midwest ends and the West begins.

Nonetheless, it would be an over-simplification to say that Nebraskans have been the helpless pawns of their environment. The state was settled by native Americans from the Midwest and the East, and—equally important—by a multitude of Europeans seeking land of their own and political freedom. Few people came here to make a fast buck. They came to stay; and most of them did.

From our early experiences gradually emerged the growing awareness that Nebraska had everything needed for both a successful agricultural and a successful industrial enterprise. During the last three decades, through collective action of individuals and various levels of government, we have made wiser use of our basic resources. If it is true that the splendid story of the pioneers is finished, it is also true that there always have been new frontiers, new demands and challenges, for Nebraskans to face and conquer.

The focus of this book, then, is on the Great Plains environment as found in Nebraska and the way that countless Nebraskans, known and unknown, responded to these conditions—politically, economically, and socially—over a span of time running back for more than a hundred years. The record speaks for itself, and Nebraskans have every reason to take pride in it.

Preparation of this volume has involved the cooperation and assistance of many individuals. I wish to acknowledge, with grateful thanks, a grant from the Nebraska Centennial Commission; and the assistance of Dr. James C. Olson, Dean of the Graduate College, Research Administrator, and Professor of History at the University of Nebraska [now Chancellor of the University of Missouri–Kansas City]; of the Nebraska State Historical Society, particularly Dr. Marvin F. Kivett, Director, and Donald F. Danker, Historian [now Professor of History, Washburn University, Topeka]; and of many other governmental agencies, museums, art galleries, photographers, and newspapers.

B. H. N.

FOREWORD TO THE BICENTENNIAL EDITION

History in formation, like the earth in upheaval during a temblor, has no distinct peaks and valleys. The events that will remain high points on history's terrain are not always clear in short perspective. This new edition of NE-BRASKA: A PICTORIAL HISTORY retains the main emphases and the body of Bruce Nicoll's work. But since the book first appeared in 1967 mankind has been given a new look at the planet it inhabits. In photographs made by astronauts on Moon missions the Earth was seen as a rich jewel held in its spatial setting by mystic forces. And with the triumphs of space exploration came technological advances in manufacturing, agriculture, medicine, and other areas of scientific endeavor.

Nebraskans, long partners of nature (though sometimes its adversaries), joined in national movements to preserve the ecosystem: the jewel in space was a garden well worth tending. As well as prizing their varied environment, Nebraskans also were attuned to the richness and potential of human life. Many, particularly young people, protested the war in Southeast Asia. Racial minorities clamored for economic and social equality and made strides toward their goals. Women emerged as leaders in government and in fields once viewed as exclusively male domains. Young and old turned to the visual, performing, and literary arts with such enthusiasm that the state has witnessed a genuine cultural renaissance.

Expanding the original volume to portray these and other recent developments, we have carried the story of Nebraska from its beginnings up to the year that the nation enters its third century. To those whose words and pictures recorded history in the making we say thanks. To those whose hands turn these pages we express the hope that a retrospective glance at Nebraska's past will help to put its present situation in focus and inspire optimism for its future.

G. M. S.

Contents

PICTURE CREDITS

All illustrations from the Nebraska State Historical Society except those listed below. Symbols are: (L) left, (R) right, (C) center, (T) top, (B) bottom. The figures indicate the page number.

Ak-Sar-Ben, 203 (TL, B); Amato, Omaha, 2; Louise Baugher, Cover; Gene Blackledge, 231 (TL); James S. Blackman, 238 (B); Burlington Northern, 58 (L), 182 (T), 209 (T); Neale Copple, 238 (T); Creighton University, 223 (T); Division of Nebraska Resources, 202 (B), 204 (C), 204 (B), 212 (T); Downey's Midwest Studio, Scottsbluff, 215 (B); Laverne Duemey, 8; Thomas Gilcrease Institute of American History and Art, 12, 13, 27 (B), 34–35; Hastings College, 222 (C); Joslyn Art Museum (Northern Natural Gas Company Collection), 17, 18 (T), 21 (all), 22–23 (T); Courtesy Sheriff Merle Karnopp, 215 (T); Kearney State College, 222 (B); Hans Knopf, courtesy of *Saturday Evening Post*, copyright 1958 by Curtis Publishing Company, 231 (BL); Jill Krementz, courtesy of Harper & Row, 231 (TR); Library of Congress, 176 (both), 177, 185; Lincoln Journal and Star Newspapers, 183 (T), 184 (T), 187 (B), 190 (both), 191 (both), 197 (T), 203 (R), 205 (T), 208 (T), 219, 240 (B); Danny Liska, 234, 237 (all); Loup River Public Power and Irrigation District, 181; Market 8 Advertising Agency, 206 (T); Montana State Historical Society, 37; Museum of Fine Arts of Houston, Texas, 47; National Aeronautics and Space Administration, 192, 195 (C), 205 (B); National Archives, 150 (B); National Park Service, 36 (B); Nebraska Educational Television Commission, 226, 227 (both); Nebraska Farmer Company, 194 (BL), 198 (BL), 198 (BR); Nebraska Public Power District, 213 (B); Nebraska State Fair, 228 (both); Nebraska Wesleyan University, 222 (T); Nebraska Wheat Commission, 200–201; Omaha Airport Authority, 207 (B); Omaha Chamber of Commerce, 207 (B), 213 (T), 229 (B); Omaha Public Library, 55 (T); Omaha *World-Herald*, 186, 230 (B) photo by Robert Pakasch and Ed Rath, 239 (T); Remote Sensing Center, Conservation and Survey Division, 194 (BR); Gilbert M. Savery, 199, 207 (T), 210 (B), 214 (both), 229 (T); Sidney *Telegraph* photo by David Hendee, 210 (T); Bernice Slote, 231 (BR); Smithsonian Institution, 98 (T); South Dakota State College, 69–73 (all); Southeast Nebraska Technical Community College, 225 (T); State Department of Roads, 183 (B), 211; State Game Commission, 195 (T), 198 (T), 202 (T), 204 (T), 230 (T), 232–33, 235 (both), 236 (both); Strategic Air Command, Omaha, 239 (B); Union Pacific Railroad Company, 42 (T), 42–43, 58 (R), 101 (B), 182 (B), 208 (B), 209 (B); United States Bureau of Reclamation, 188; USDA–Soil Conservation Service, 179 (all), 184 (BR), 195 (TR), 196; University of Nebraska Medical Center, 223 (B); University of Nebraska–Lincoln, 187 (TL), 187 (TR), 194 (T), 197 (B), 220, 221 (T), 224 (both); University of Nebraska at Omaha, 221 (B); Walters Art Gallery, Baltimore, 22 (B), 22–23 (T), 23 (B); Nebraska Western College, 225 (B); Whitney Gallery, Cody, Wyoming, 120; Don M. Wright, 216 (all), 217, 218 (all). Maps by Jack Brodie, 11, 15, 24, 32, 55, 212.

Mitchell Pass, in Scotts Bluff County, was the gateway to the Rocky Mountains for tens of thousands of emigrants on the way west.

THE WAY WEST
(To 1854)

The land that would one day be Nebraska came into the possession of the young American republic in 1803, with the sale and transfer from France to the United States of the half billion acres of wilderness lying between the Mississippi River and the Rocky Mountains. Spanish explorers had first penetrated this vast land mass more than two and a half centuries before the Louisiana Purchase, but the Spaniards, like the French who came after them, were itinerants—traders and exploiters, not colonizers.

Signalizing the advent of the United States sovereignty—and a portent of mighty things to come—was the Lewis and Clark Expedition (1803–1806), which demonstrated the feasibility of an overland route to the Pacific and opened the door to American expansion westward. The republic was manifestly destined to extend from sea to sea, but in the early 1840's, when the first massive waves of migration began to roll west, men's eyes were set beyond the mountains to the Oregon country. The area between the Missouri and the Rockies, according to a succession of government reports, was a desert, "almost wholly unfit for cultivation," of interest and significance chiefly because the way to the Promised Land led through it.

What was to be the road from the Missouri River to the foothills of the Rockies on the Oregon Trail—the most famous emigration route in American history—was discovered by a fur trader, Robert Stuart, in 1813, and defined in 1830 by the wagons of the fur-trading firm of Smith, Jackson, and Sublette. Leaving the Santa Fe Trail in Kansas about forty miles west of Independence, Missouri, it angled northwestward across the undulating prairies bordering the Blue and the Platte rivers. The vast grassland provided forage for the horses, cows, and oxen of the emigrants; the trees along these rivers provided fuel for their campfires; the streams provided life-giving water. Nature had fashioned the broad valley of the Platte into one of the world's great highways; through the land that was to become Nebraska lay *the* way west.

The First Inhabitants

Archeological and other scientific findings attest that Nebraska was inhabited as far back as ten thousand years ago, but it has not yet been determined if these prehistoric peoples were the ancestors of the Indians that the white man encountered on the northern plains. Among the historic tribes, the Pawnees, a semi-sedentary farming people who lived in permanent villages but made periodic trips to hunt the buffalo, were most closely identified with Nebraska. In the east along the Missouri dwelt the sedentary Siouan tribes—Omahas, Poncas, Otos, Iowas, and Missourias—and roaming the western lands were the nomadic tribes, hunting people who lived in tipis, of whom the most important in Nebraska's history were the Brules and Oglalas, subtribes of the Teton Sioux (Dakotas); the Cheyennes; and the Arapahos.

From ancient dwelling sites archeologists of the State Historical Society are reconstructing the culture of Nebraska's earliest inhabitants. The campsite in Burt County, left, dates back nine thousand years. The pottery and the effigy pipe were used in Nebraska hundreds of years ago.

About 1650 A.D. an early Pawnee earth lodge village in Nance County was destroyed by hostile Indians. This reconstruction, based on archeological research by the State Historical Society, shows the initial phase of the siege.

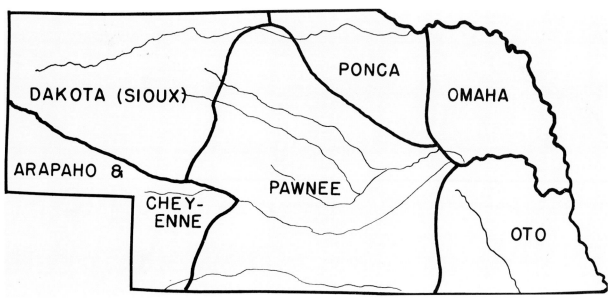

Indian tribes in Nebraska about 1800

The horse tremendously assisted the Indian in hunting his chief source of meat, the buffalo.

Horses, first brought to the Great Plains by the Spanish explorers, proliferated rapidly and provided the Nebraska Indian with transportation to move his villages.

The Indian became a skilled mounted warrior, equipped with knives, spears, bows, and arrows, able to strike swiftly and unexpectedly. In the ceaseless warfare between the Plains tribes, the horse became the prized plunder of the victor.

Here are the dwellings of the Nebraska Indians as seen by the white man's camera in 1870: the tipis of the Southern Cheyennes, a nomadic tribe; and the earth lodges of the Pawnees, a semi-sedentary tribe.

The Pathfinders

Exploration of the Great Plains began less than fifty years after the discovery of America. It was in 1541 that gold-seeking Spanish soldiers led by the conquistador Francisco Vásquez de Coronado marched north from Mexico in search of the mythical Kingdom of Quivira. Their quest took them as far as central Kansas where, instead of golden cities, they found the grass huts of the Wichita Indians. A century and a quarter later the French began to infiltrate the Plains region coming up the Missouri, and by 1723 Étienne de Bourgmont, a *coureur de bois*, had established a fort in the vicinity of present Brunswick, Missouri. (Bourgmont's reference to a river "called Nibraskier" is the first recorded use of the term.) Meanwhile Spain's interest in the region had been rekindled by news of French activity, and in 1720 an expedition under Pedro de Villasur got as far north as the Platte River before being all but wiped out in an Indian attack. It remained for two Frenchmen, Pierre and Paul Mallet, to open the way to Santa Fe, a feat they accomplished in 1739. The expedition got off to an inauspicious start: the brothers believed they could reach New Mexico by following the Missouri, and didn't change their minds until they had gone up river to the mouth of the Niobrara. Heading back overland they eventually came to—and named—the Platte, followed it to the Loup fork, crossed the river there, and trekked southwest until they reached the Arkansas. An Indian guided them the rest of the way to Santa Fe.

With the opening of the nineteenth century came the most significant accomplishment in the exploration of the West: the Lewis and Clark Expedition from St. Louis to the mouth of the Columbia River. Lewis and Clark's route took them along the eastern and northeastern boundaries of Nebraska; two subsequent government expeditions—one led by Lieutenant Zebulon M. Pike in 1806, the other by Major Stephen H. Long in 1820—passed through the southern part of the future state. After Pike's report of "barren soil, parched and dried up for eight months of the year" and Long's opinion that the region was "uninhabitable by a people depending on agriculture for their subsistence," the land between the Missouri and the Rockies became generally known as the Great American Desert. It would take more than a generation to get the matter straightened out.

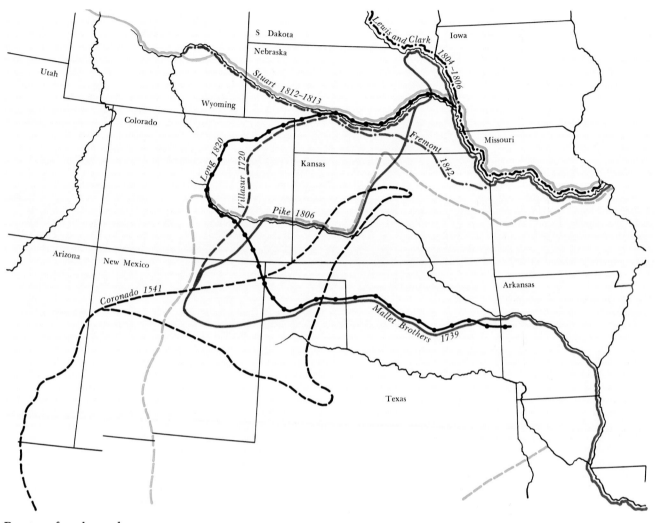

Routes of early explorers

Captain Meriwether Lewis

Captain William Clark

Major Stephen H. Long's expedition up the Platte and South Platte to the Rockies in 1820 confirmed the report made in 1806 by Lieutenant Zebulon M. Pike that the region was a wasteland, fit only for nomadic savages. Shown above is Long's meeting with the Pawnee Indian Council.

Lieutenant Zebulon M. Pike

Major Stephen H. Long

Fur Traders and European Visitors

On the trans-Missouri frontier, as on many new frontiers, fur trading was the first big business. After the French lost their stake in the North American continent, British firms—notably the Hudson's Bay Company—dominated the trade until challenged by the Americans in the early nineteenth century. The fur business was important not only in its economic aspects, but for its role in opening up a new country. Hunters and traders necessarily were also explorers; and the company trading posts, where they brought their pelts and purchased supplies, were the first permanent settlements. In 1812, Manuel Lisa of the Missouri Fur Company, who five years earlier had led the first trading expedition to the upper Missouri, established what became the most important Nebraska post, Fort Lisa near the Council Bluff. Such distinguished visitors from overseas as the explorer-prince, Maximilian von Wied-Neuwied, and the Scottish sportsman Captain William Drummond Stewart were entertained at Bellevue, the American Fur Company post a few miles down river.

After 1831 the fur-trading post at Bellevue was operated by Peter A. Sarpy. Manuel Lisa is said to have named the site in 1807. Shown above is the Indian agency of Major John Dougherty, as sketched by Carl Bodmer in 1833.

The steamer *Yellowstone* carried Prince Maximilian and his party on the eighteen-hundred-mile journey from St. Louis to Fort Union, the fur-trading capital of the upper Missouri.

Manuel Lisa   Peter A. Sarpy   Prince Maximilian von Wied-Neuwied   Captain William Drummond Stewart

Bullboats, light rawhide craft which could be portaged and which were best suited to the Platte's shallow waters, transported furs from the mountains to posts on the Missouri. There they were loaded on flat boats called mackinaws and shipped down to St. Louis. Robidoux Post, shown below, was an important fur-trading center in western Nebraska.

In 1823, Bellevue, the oldest white settlement in Nebraska, succeeded Fort Atkinson as an Indian agency serving the Omaha, Oto, Missouria, and Pawnee tribes. It is seen above as it looked in 1858.

To teach the gospel and to rescue the redman from the fur trader's firewater, missionaries came to Nebraska in the early 1830's. The first sermon was preached by Moses Merrill, a Baptist, in 1833 at Bellevue. This is the Presbyterian mission there in 1854.

After the War of 1812, forts went up along the Missouri to protect the fur trade from the Indians and to keep an eye on British beaver men. The westernmost army post in the U.S. was Fort Atkinson, near present Omaha, built in 1820 and abandoned in 1827. Bodmer painted its ruins in 1833.

Bodmer's portraits of Indians document the Nebraska Indian's appearance before his way of life was reshaped by the white man. Three of his subjects are shown at the right.

Oto Indian   Omaha child   Ponca chief

When Captain William Drummond Stewart visited the Plains and the Rockies in 1837, his party included twenty gentlemen, thirty hunters, muleteers, servants, and an artist, Alfred Jacob Miller. Here is Miller's view of Scotts Bluff.

Stewart's colorful caravan, which, surprisingly enough, was not once molested by Indians, is shown in another of Miller's paintings crossing the Platte.

The enormous herds of buffalo, seen here watering at night on the Platte, never ceased to impress Stewart's party.

In 1837 Alfred J. Miller, fascinated by the Oregon Trail, made this painting of Chimney Rock, perhaps Nebraska's most famous landmark.

The Overland Trails

Land of their own, freedom from religious persecution, the chance of quick riches in the gold fields—these were among the motives that impelled men westward during the first decade of the Great Migration. In 1841, only about eighty emigrants crossed the plains; in 1843, the number jumped to more than a thousand; in 1847, six thousand traversed the Oregon Trail, and another two thousand bound for Salt Lake City, the new Zion, followed Brigham Young over the Mormon Trail on the north side of the Platte. Then in 1848 came the discovery of gold in California, and it is estimated that during the next two summers more than a hundred thousand men and women dared the crossing. As the trail filled up, grass and game became scarce; cholera and other diseases ravaged the emigrant trains; Indian attacks were constantly dreaded and occasionally materialized. But hopes outweighed hazards, and year after year the wagons rolled westward.

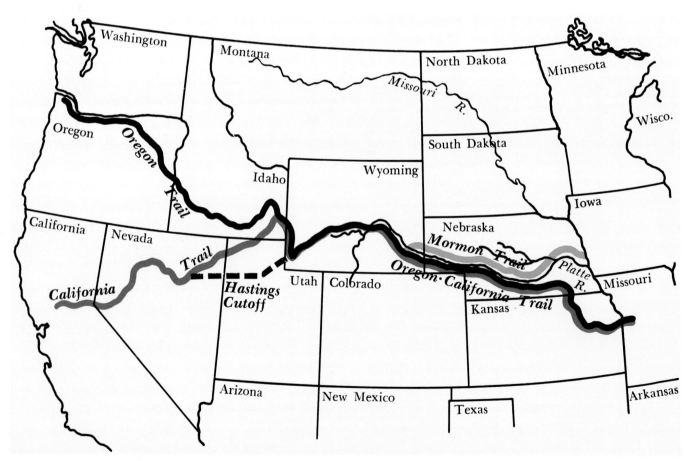

Overland trails through Nebraska

The Oregon Trail entered Nebraska at about the Jefferson-Gage county line and angled northwest along the valley of the Little Blue. Rock Creek was the first station.

Near Fort Kearny the trail was littered with the jettisoned belongings of overloaded emigrants. Others, insufficiently equipped, had to ask the Army for supplies.

Because of the profusion of flowers, the route along the Platte west of Fort Kearny was nicknamed "The Sunflower Trail."

After following the Platte to its fork, the Oregon Trail moved along the South Platte to a point seven miles east of Big Springs, where the river was forded.

For the sport of it, Indians occasionally stampeded a buffalo herd into a wagon train. If the wagons stood in their path, the huge, frightened beasts drove straight into them.

Wagon breakdowns could lead to disastrous delays; and cholera and other diseases took thousands of lives. Yet the overriding fear was of Indian attacks.

In the early phase of the Mormon migration from Winter Quarters (near Omaha) to Salt Lake City, Brigham Young provided wagon transportation for his followers. When funds ran out the faithful were asked to foot it, pulling handcarts.

Chimney Rock, jutting up from the Platte Valley, told the emigrant that the long trek across the prairie was nearing its end.

At Mitchell Pass the overlanders left Nebraska. The trail ahead in the high plains and mountains would be tougher going.

TERRITORY TO STATE
(1854-1870)

As the second half of the nineteenth century opened, although the Far West and the Southwest were organized—California and Texas were states; Washington, Oregon, Utah, and New Mexico were territories—the inland empire stretching west from the banks of the Missouri to the Pacific side of the Rockies was still almost devoid of settlement. From the 1820's on, government policy toward the trans-Missouri country had been shaped by the reports of Long and other explorers: Since the area was unfit for agriculture, let it be used as a dumping ground for the Indian tribes displaced by white occupation of the Mississippi Valley. But the idea of a "permanent Indian frontier" could not prevail against the pressure of the westward-moving pioneer and the tide of manifest destiny.

The West's desire to be linked to the Union, the agitation for a transcontinental railroad, the controversy over the extension of slavery, and the clamor raised by "Nebraska Boomers"—whose accounts of the area's climate and soil contradicted the "Great American Desert" myth—were the major forces behind the passage of the Kansas-Nebraska Act, signed by President Pierce on May 30, 1854. Nebraska Territory, which now came into being, was a whopper, extending from the Missouri to the crest of the Rockies, and from the fortieth parallel north to the Canadian border. The Act provided that all questions pertaining to slavery in the territory were to be "left to the decision of the people residing therein, through their appropriate representatives," and it initiated the process that would extinguish Indian titles to the land and confine the tribes to much smaller tracts. Thus, in 1854, with the extension of territorial organization to all the remaining lands of the Louisiana Purchase, the concept of "Indian country" west of the Missouri was ended forever and the way was opened for white settlement from coast to coast.

Politicians and Politics

Nebraska's territorial history opened on a note of somber melodrama: Francis Burt of South Carolina, who had been appointed governor by President Pierce, was desperately ill when he reached Bellevue, and died on October 18, two days after the oath of office had been administered at his bedside. Secretary Thomas B. Cuming served as Acting Governor until the arrival of Burt's successor, Mark W. Izard, on February 20, 1855.

All the problems confronting the early legislators—chartering banks, organizing the public schools, securing land titles to the settlers, devising a constitution—had to be resolved in the heat of the bitter sectional strife between those living north of the Platte River and those living south of it. The territory had been created under a Democratic administration, and the first legislature contained twenty-seven Democrats and twelve Whigs; but by 1862, with Lincoln in the White House and the Civil War raging, the Republican party had gained the ascendancy.

Francis Burt
First Territorial Governor
(1854)

Thomas B. Cuming
Acting Territorial Governor
(1854)

Mark W. Izard
Second Territorial Governor
(1854–1857)

Alvin Saunders
Last Territorial Governor
(1861–1867)

David Butler
First State Governor
(1867–1871)

J. Sterling Morton
"Nebraska Boomer"
and Territorial Leader

31

Bellevue, seen here about 1856, had high hopes
of becoming the territorial capital.

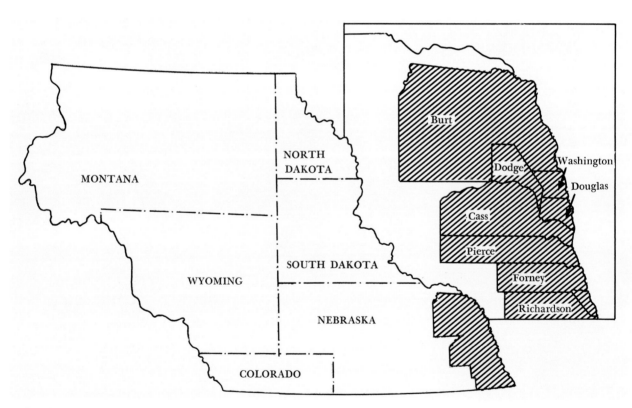

Nebraska counties on a territorial map in 1854,
thirteen years before statehood came

Iowa promoters, hoping to improve their chances of securing the Pacific railroad route through Council Bluffs, influenced Governor Cuming to name Omaha the Nebraska capital. The first territorial legislature convened there on January 16, 1855, in the capitol building shown above. A new building, the second and last territorial capitol, was completed in 1858.

The Transportation Boom

Traffic on the overland trails, which began to slack off in 1853, picked up dramatically after 1857, partly because of a series of gold and silver strikes in Arizona, Colorado, Nevado, Idaho, and Montana, each one of which meant a rush to the new diggings, and partly because of the skyrocketing demand for goods of all kinds in the western settlements and military posts. Responding to the need for more and speedier means of transportation and communication, freight lines and stage lines came into being, and until the telegraph and the railroad permanently altered the picture, the bullwhacker, stagecoach driver, and Pony Express rider were ubiquitous and prominent figures on the Nebraska scene. Steamboat traffic, which reached its peak in 1859, also was vitally important to the transportation system in pre-Iron Horse days. The arrival of the first boat up river each spring was celebrated by the entire population of the Nebraska river towns at the eastern end of the Great Platte Valley Road.

During the 1850's and '60's the brilliantly hued overland stagecoach, bouncing and swaying over the trail with mail and passengers, was at least as glamorous a sight as the jet liner would be a century later. In 1851 the government contract for the first through mail service between Independence and Sacramento called for monthly mail delivery, but the schedule was seldom kept. In 1862 the Butterfield Overland Mail was purchased by Ben Holladay, who greatly improved the service, and in 1866 ownership passed to Wells Fargo, which operated the line until the completion of the Pacific railroad. Subsequently, the coaches were used only for local service. The average speed of the overland stage was six miles per hour, upped to ten over the relatively smooth Platte Valley leg of the route. Stagecoach travel was not cheap; in 1865, the fare from the Missouri River to Denver was $175. Indian attacks were by no means unknown, but virtually all the coaches got through safely.

In April, 1860, the nation was electrified by the news that the Pony Express, established by the firm of Russell, Majors and Waddell, had carried the mail between St. Joseph and Sacramento in ten days—half the time taken by the stagecoach. The riders worked in relays of about a hundred miles each, picking up fresh mounts at way stations every ten to twelve miles.

As construction of the telegraph moved west from the Missouri and east from California, the Pony Express route progressively shortened. Though it operated for only nineteen months, the Pony Express demonstrated the practicability of the central route for the railroad and helped bind the West to the Union cause during the opening months of the Civil War.

The deadline for completing the telegraph line west to Salt Lake City was July 31, 1862. Despite incredible supply problems, Edward Creighton, later prominently identified with Omaha's growth, finished the job on October 20, 1861, and the lines were joined four days later. Listening to the hum of the talking wires, the Indian was mystified and worried by this new encroachment on his domain.

Mining camps, army posts, and the growing settlements of the West relied on freighting firms for their supplies. A standard "bull outfit," with a crew of around 30 men and 300 to 320 oxen, consisted of 25 freight wagons and a mess wagon. Pictured above are army supply wagons bucking a Great Plains blizzard, as seen by a New York newspaper correspondent.

The biggest freighting firm on the Plains was Russell, Majors and Waddell. When they established a terminal at Nebraska City in 1857, a sleepy frontier settlement was transformed into a bustling town.

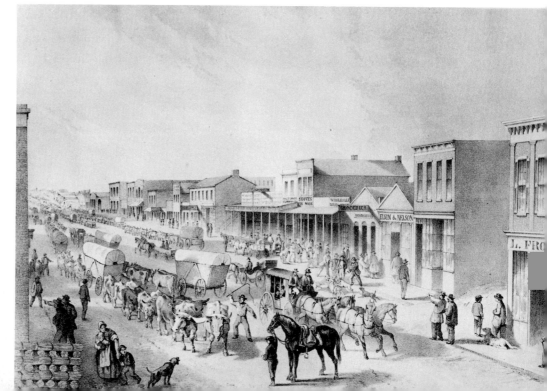

A wagon freight train near Fort Kearny yokes up its oxen for another long day on the road. In the distance an overland stage with escort follows the Platte road, now marked out by telegraph poles.

River traffic boomed throughout the 1850's. At Nebraska City, a major port of call, huge quantities of freight were unloaded on the docks for transfer to the westbound wagons.

During the heyday of the river trade, arrivals at the Omaha levee averaged a steamboat daily. In this 1868 drawing the crowd watches the docking of the *Jennie Brown*, whose route took her upstream as far as Fort Benton.

The *Red Cloud* was typical of the shallow-draft
steamers which plied the Big Muddy in the
1860's.

Sectional rivalry over the route of the Pacific railroad held up the project throughout the 1850's, but the Civil War put an end to the long debate. On July 1, 1862, Congress chartered the Union Pacific to build a road from Omaha to Utah, and provided aid to the Central Pacific to build the western end. The war held up construction—only forty miles of track had been laid in eastern Nebraska by the end of 1865 (above)—but after that, with plenty of men, money, and supplies available, the rails fairly leaped westward through the Platte Valley. On May 10, 1869, the Union Pacific and the Central Pacific met at Promontory Point, near Ogden, Utah, and iron rails now bound the nation together.

Track-laying gangs, mostly Irish immigrants and discharged soldiers, were supplied by work trains, as illustrated below. These trains shuttled back and forth between end-of-track and supply points farther east. This scene is in western Nebraska.

Until 1867, when the Chicago and North Western tracks reached Council Bluffs from Chicago, Union Pacific construction supplies were shipped up the Missouri from St. Louis. This is the U.P. Omaha landing in 1865.

Passenger service west on the Union Pacific was available almost as soon as the track went down. At end-of-track, passengers transferred to overland stage to complete their journey. This is the Omaha depot in 1868.

The Homestead Act

The American dream of free land on the western frontier was realized when President Lincoln signed the Homestead Act on May 20, 1862. Although it was amended many times, chiefly to extend its privileges, basically the Act provided that any person who was the head of a family or over twenty-one, was a U.S. citizen or intended to become one, and had never borne arms against the government could claim up to quarter-section of land on payment of a $10 filing fee. When he had proved up on his claim—lived on it or cultivated it for the five years immediately following filing—he secured a final patent on the land. Ultimately the Act brought more than a hundred thousand homesteaders into Nebraska, but in 1862 the nation was in the grip of the Civil War and the great land rush did not begin until the next decade.

Daniel Freeman, home on furlough from the Union Army, filed the first entry in the United States under the terms of the Homestead Act on New Year's Day, 1863, then left to rejoin his regiment. This painting shows Freeman in later years.

The Indian Problem

Stated in its simplest terms, the Indian problem was the age-old one that always arose when one people moved in on another and took over its lands: Where were the dispossessed to go? The answer, so the government thought, was the reservation system.

In 1857, when the Pawnees ceded their remaining lands in Nebraska and agreed to accept a reservation on the Loup fork, Indian holdings in the eastern half of the future state were reduced to a few small tracts. The farming tribes of the east, even before the territorial period, had been generally friendly and easy to deal with; in the west, domain of the warlike nomadic tribes, it was a different story. Although in 1851, under the terms of the Horse Creek treaty, the Indians of the northern plains recognized the government's right to establish roads and military posts through their lands, unrest was constant on both sides and it flamed into open warfare in 1854. After General Harney's 1855 punitive expedition, the tribes were fairly peaceful until the summer of 1862, when six years of hostilities began with the uprising of the Santee Sioux in Minnesota. The 2nd Nebraska Cavalry was organized to meet the threat and the following year helped to crush the Santees at White Stone Hill (in present North Dakota). But in the west, particularly in the summers of 1864 and 1865, the Teton Sioux, Cheyennes, and Arapahos, again and again attacked stage stations, emigrant trains, and road ranches all the way from Denver to the Little Blue Valley. An uneasy peace was negotiated at Fort Laramie in 1868, and some of the hostile chiefs accepted the principle of fixed reservations, but the Indian problem was still a long way from being solved.

Made apprehensive by the increasing activity on the overland trails and determined to preserve the lands guaranteed to him by treaty, the Indian's reaction was simple and direct. He attacked the intruders.

Fort Kearny, located on the big bend of the Platte, was established in 1848 to protect overland emigrants. For more than twenty years it was one of the best-known points on the Oregon Trail.

Fort McPherson, just east of the forks of the Platte, was established in 1863 by the 7th Iowa Cavalry, sent west when it was feared the Confederates were organizing a general Indian uprising.

On September 3, 1863, the 2nd Nebraska Cavalry under Colonel Robert W. Furnas joined with General Alfred Sully's 6th Iowa Cavalry in wiping out a Sioux encampment at White Stone Hill. The drawing is by an eye-witness.

Sidney Barracks, later Fort Sidney, was built in 1867 after peace negotiations had failed the preceding year and the Indians continued their hit-and-run harassment of Platte Valley travelers.

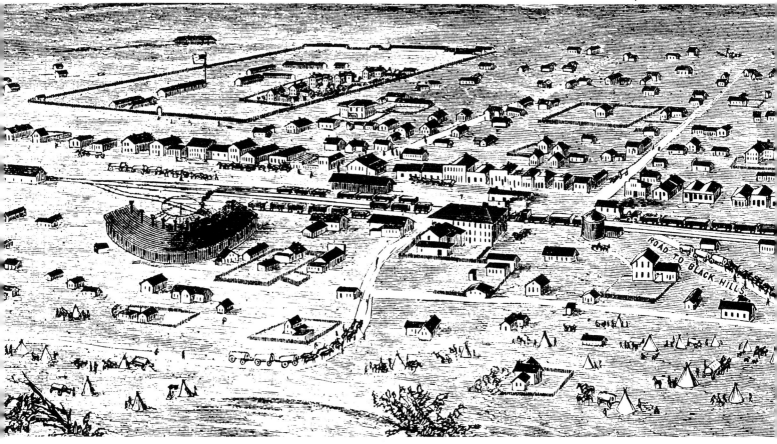

To the redman it seemed a final threat to his existence when steel rails began cutting through his hunting country, and attacks on construction crews were frequent. Much of the U.P. construction in Nebraska was carried on under the protection of U.S. troops, including Major Frank North's famous Pawnee Scouts.

In 1868, a Peace Commission met at Fort Laramie with Red Cloud and other hostile Plains Indian chiefs. The treaty they signed provided that the area north of the North Platte and east of the Big Horns was to be regarded as unceded Indian territory, and that the part of present South Dakota west of the Missouri River was to be a Sioux reservation. The U.S. agreed to abandon Forts Reno, C. F. Smith, and Phil Kearny in Wyoming, and to close the Bozeman Road (which ran through the Sioux hunting grounds to the mining camps in Montana). But despite these concessions, there were many so-called non-treaty Sioux, among them Sitting Bull and Crazy Horse, who refused to recognize the Fort Laramie proceedings.

The Thirty-Seventh State

Nebraska's progress toward statehood was accompanied by a good deal of backing and filling, largely the result of maneuvering by politicians who were less concerned with how soon Nebraska was admitted to the Union than that this should take place when they had the best chance of becoming officeholders.

Agitation for immediate statehood began as early as 1858 and in 1859 everybody seemed to be for it. When the voters went to the polls in March, 1860, however, the result showed they had changed their minds. In January, 1864, the legislature sought congressional authorization to form a state government and the Enabling Act was passed the following April. But when the constitutional convention met in July, the delegates were overwhelmingly opposed to statehood and promptly adjourned. In January, 1866, Governor Alvin Saunders, who was determined to get action, proposed that the legislature itself adopt a constitution. Drafted in secret by a bipartisan committee, the document was rammed through the legislature and submitted to the voters in June. It squeaked by with a margin of one hundred votes; in the same election David Butler was named governor.

At this point another hitch developed. Like most state constitutions at this time, the Nebraska constitution denied the right to vote to non-whites, and Congress eventually amended the bill for Nebraska's statehood to provide that it would not take effect until the restriction had been eliminated. The bill was passed over President Andrew Johnson's veto on February 9, 1867. On February 20 the legislature, meeting in special session, nullified the restrictive provision by declaring that "white in their constitution meant any color whatsoever," and on March 1 the President signed the proclamation admitting Nebraska to the Union.

During the territorial years Nebraska's physical size shrank by nearly four-fifths: Colorado and Dakota territories were carved out of it in 1861, and Idaho (including present Wyoming and Montana) in 1863. At the time of its admission to the Union, Nebraska included 75,995 square miles. Later changes, the most important being the annexation of the Sioux reserve (now Boyd County) in 1890, brought the state to its present area of 77,237 square miles.

This was the homestead home of Judge Luke Lavender in 1867. Lavender's was one of a half-dozen log cabins comprising the village of Lancaster when a commission chose it as the site of the state capital, to be known thereafter as Lincoln.

Nebraska's capital city about 1868. In the background is the salt basin which, it was once believed, had great potential value. Captain W. T. Donovan, who came to the area in 1856, was one of many who were disappointed in their hopes of making a fortune in salt.

Because of the probability that the seat of government would be located elsewhere if the capitol building were not ready for the first meeting of the state legislature on January 1, 1869, the work was rushed to completion on December 1, 1868, at a cost of nearly twice the $40,000 appropriated.

This was Omaha in 1867. The city, which had long cherished the hope of becoming the state capital, lost its bid when the south-of-Platte legislators voted the straight sectional ticket. The building at the extreme left was the second territorial capitol building.

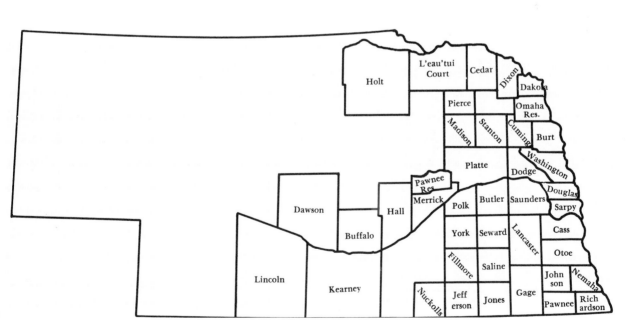

Nebraska counties in 1865, two years before statehood

THE TESTING YEARS
(1870-1900)

In Nebraska the last third of the nineteenth century was a period of dramatic growth and of adaptation to the peculiar demands of the Great Plains environment. Life for settlers in the new state began auspiciously enough with good crops during the early years of the 1870's. But then the roof fell in. In 1873 a financial panic swept the nation. Prices for farm products dropped, and, as the crisis deepened, some Nebraska farmers could find no market for their crops. The terrible blizzard of April, 1873, known as the Easter Storm, caused great loss of life and property. And then came searing drouth and the grasshopper invasions—three years when hordes of locusts blackened the sky and destroyed every growing thing. Relief in the form of food and clothing was shipped in from the eastern states and dispensed by aid societies and the Army, but many homesteaders gave up the struggle and went back to their homes in the east.

By 1877 the rains had returned and the scourge of grasshoppers disappeared. Now those who had stuck it out had their reward, for the 1880's were a period of great prosperity. In the words of an early historian, Addison E. Sheldon, this decade saw "the largest addition to our population; the greatest increase in our production; the furthest extension of railroad mileage; the greatest change in the physical aspects of our state." Not only was more land taken up by settlers, more livestock added, and more new towns founded, but "more schools were created, more churches built, and more homes constructed than in any other decade of Nebraska history."

The Homesteaders

Thousands of families from the eastern states and a dozen European countries poured into Nebraska during the settlement years. Millions of acres of land was the great prize, but it took some doing to claim it. Whether the settler came from back east or abroad, he had been used to farming in regions where water and timber were plentiful. In Nebraska he found a vast ocean of grass with only occasional groves of trees clinging to the banks of shallow streams which dried up to a trickle during the periodic drouths. To survive, the settler had to innovate—to improvise solutions with the materials at hand—and to apply technological advances. When there was no wood for cabins, he carved his home out of the prairie sod and dwelt in a dugout or a soddy, he used buffalo chips for fuel; he sank deep wells and harnessed the Nebraska wind to pump his water. He licked the fencing problem when barbed wire was put on the market in 1874; and he successfully developed the cultivation practices known as dryland farming.

The homesteader had brought with him the crops he knew and understood in the east—corn, spring wheat, rye, and barley. In the 1890's, alfalfa came into general use, as did sugar beets. Livestock numbers increased rapidly in the late 1890's, and a serum for hog cholera reduced the losses from the disease. Although the outlook for agriculture was good, one observer warned that "The time has come when the farmer must mix brains with his toil, or fall to the rear." Farm mechanization and the infant stage of science's entrance into farming were close at hand.

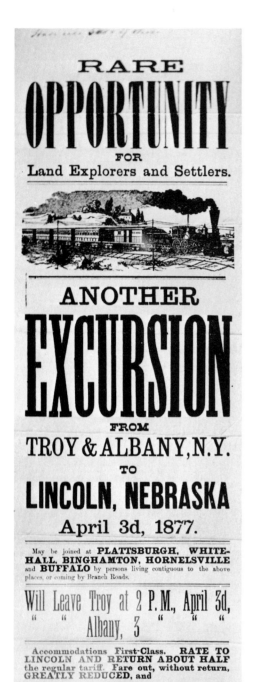

The Burlington and Missouri Railroad, which started building westward from Plattsmouth in 1869 and reached Lincoln in 1870, followed a route along the Republican Valley and extended to Benkelman, near the Colorado border, by the end of 1881. To help pay for construction, the Burlington was granted 2,415,000 acres of land from the state and federal governments; earlier, the Union Pacific had received 4,850,000 acres. With such a stake in the country, the railroads joined the state government in a large-scale promotional campaign to attract settlers from the East and Europe. Posters such as these were widely displayed.

Most of the landseekers from the eastern United States, as well as immigrants from the Old World, came west to Nebraska by rail.

The newcomers found temporary shelter in immigrant houses such as this one in Lincoln, maintained by the Burlington.

The homesteader traveled the last lap of his long journey in a wagon loaded with his household goods, farm implements, and personal possessions.

Frequently the settler's first home on the prairie
was a dugout.

Many homesteads were located some distance from a surface water supply and hauling water was an arduous task. This problem was overcome with the discovery of Nebraska's generous groundwater. Water at shallow depth was lifted in buckets by pulley and ropes, at deeper levels by windmills, driven by Nebraska's unceasing winds.

Overleaf: A Custer County homesteader, Solomon D. Butcher, was also an itinerant photographer, and the pictures of the Butcher Collection comprise a superb visual record of homestead life in the last quarter of the nineteenth century. When pioneering families sat for him, they arrayed themselves in their best and displayed their most prized possessions. Butcher photographs appear on pages 60 through 68.

The T. M. Bates family

The Elmer Ball family

Bachelor E. G. Alger

Unidentified lady in a straw hat

The Jerry Shore family

Bachelor Andy Howland

A sod-house school near Ord

Miss Mary Longfellow, a school teacher, was also
holding down a claim west of Broken Bow.

The Isadore Haumont family and their two-story soddy. Heirs ordered it razed in 1972.

On the page opposite and the five following pages are accurate portrayals of homestead life in the Plains region. They were painted in South Dakota by Harvey Dunn, who also supplied the titles.

Bringing Home the Bride

After the Blizzard

R.F.D.

Thirty Below

Breaking Sod

The Prairie Is My Garden

After School

Woman at the Pump

As lumber became available at reasonable prices in the 1880's, many a sodbuster built on a frame addition to his soddy.

By the 1890's, sod-house construction was disappearing in favor of all-wood buildings. Shown in this silhouette are a settler and the essentials of a new homestead: one-room house, a team of horses, a plow, the outhouse, and the cattle shed and yard.

Two-story houses with balconies became more common in the prosperous 1880's. This is the N. W. Morgan house near Callaway, in 1889.

As the century drew to a close, sod-house schools were disappearing, and one-room frame schools, the symbol of rural education, dotted the prairie. This school was in Buffalo County.

As part of their campaign to destroy the "Great American Desert" myth, promotional agencies seized on and circulated the theory that "rainfall follows the plow"—that moisture became more plentiful after the soil was broken. In fact, of course, it was the homesteader who followed the plow while turning about one million acres of Nebraska prairie, and the "increased moisture" was the sweat dripping from his brow as he toiled from dawn to dusk.

Corn, the first crop planted by the pioneers, was the state's most important crop. These pictures were taken in the lush 1880's. By the end of that decade Nebraska was producing more than a tenth of the nation's corn.

32
↓

Nebraska farmers of the 1880's and 1890's figured that swine at five dollars a hundred could be fed profitably on fifty-cent corn. For years this was popularly known as the "corn-hog ratio." The herd of "mortgage lifters" shown was photographed in Buffalo County in the late 1890's.

Alfalfa, first grown in the state in the '70's, was the major crop innovation in nineteenth-century farming in Nebraska. It was a good forage crop and a soil builder.

If, by the end of the nineteenth century, the
Nebraska homesteader was beginning to enjoy
some of the comforts of town life, he had earned
them. Equipped only with his gun, the tools and
implements with which to work the soil and
build, and his own two hands, he had solved the
problems of food and shelter and fought to preserve his farm against the ravages of prairie fires
(pictured above), drouths, blizzards, grasshopper
scourges, and other natural hazards. Even after
he had achieved a measure of reward for his
labors, his life was one of isolation and loneli-
ness, with few opportunities to foregather with
his neighbors. For him and his family, the church
and school were centers of social as well as
spiritual life.

The Cattlemen

Nebraska's cattle industry began in Texas. The long-horned cattle brought to Texas by the Spanish thrived and multiplied into vast herds—hundreds of thousands of cattle running wild, in addition to ranch herds. Following the Civil War, the scarcity of beef in the north meant boom days for the range cattle industry. A steer that sold for six dollars in Texas fetched forty or fifty in Chicago; the problem was how to get the herds to market. Since settlement blocked the trails as far west as the ninety-eighth meridian, the long trail drives awaited the coming of railroads in Kansas and Nebraska. Schuyler, at the upper end of the Blue River trail, was Nebraska's first shipping point and about 50,000 cattle were sold there in 1870. But the Blue Valley was settling up, and in 1871 trail's end shifted westward to Kearney. Two years later it moved again, this time to Ogallala, gateway to the northern Plains. For ten years Ogallala was Nebraska's cattle capital; more than 100,000 head were received there annually and shipped east over the Union Pacific.

The curtain fell on one of the most colorful phases of Western American history in the late 1880's when the Long Drive came to an end, but by that time Nebraska had developed its own thriving cattle industry. The first ranches were in the lower Panhandle between the North and South Platte; by 1900 the industry had spread to the northern and western boundaries of the state and as far east as Grand Island. Shorthorns, Herefords, and the Angus breed replaced the unsatisfactory Texas longhorn. Such men as John Bratt, William F. Cody, Captain James H. Cook, the Newman brothers, Frank and Luther North, Colonel James Pratt, Bartlett Richards, William G. Comstock, A. J. Abbott, J. M. Gentry, James Forbes, and J. H. Minor successively built up the herds that were to make Nebraska famous as "The Beef State."

As the line of homesteader settlement moved westward, the conflict of interest between the cattlemen running their herds on the open range and the homesteaders bent on fencing their small claims resulted in a number of bloody incidents. In Nebraska, however, the violence was something less than in the neighboring areas of the northern Great Plains.

Nebraska's range cattle industry began when the
Texas longhorn was driven north over the long
dusty trail to Union Pacific railheads. A trail
herd usually numbered about two thousand.

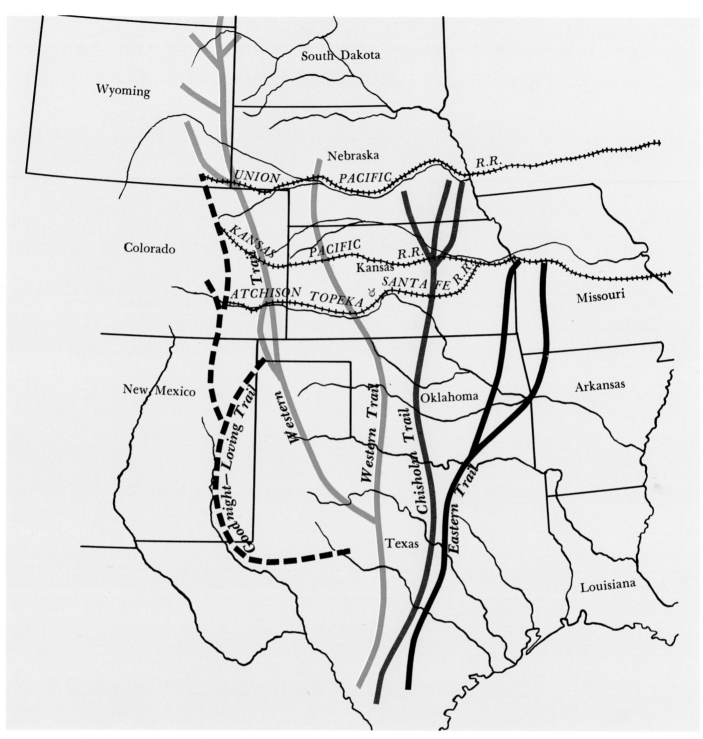

As homesteaders moved out on the plains, the
cattle trails were pushed westward. The days of
the Long Drive came to an end in the mid-1880's
when expanding settlement blocked the trails
and homesteaders invoked herd laws to keep the
cattle out.

The Union Pacific shipping points were, successively, Schuyler, Kearney, and Ogallala. Here the steers were driven up chutes into cattle cars which conveyed them to packers in Omaha and Chicago.

The sinister tales told of the mysterious Sandhills caused white men and Indians alike to dread the region. Then in April, 1879, men of the Newman ranch braved the interior in search of cattle driven past the line-riders during a blizzard the previous winter. To their surprise they found their cattle all thriving, and, more importantly, they discovered lush grass and numerous lakes in this supposedly arid country. Conclusive proof that the best range in the West had been overlooked came in the blizzard-ridden winter of 1880–1881, when thousands of cattle died in the Platte Valley while losses in the Sandhills were negligible.

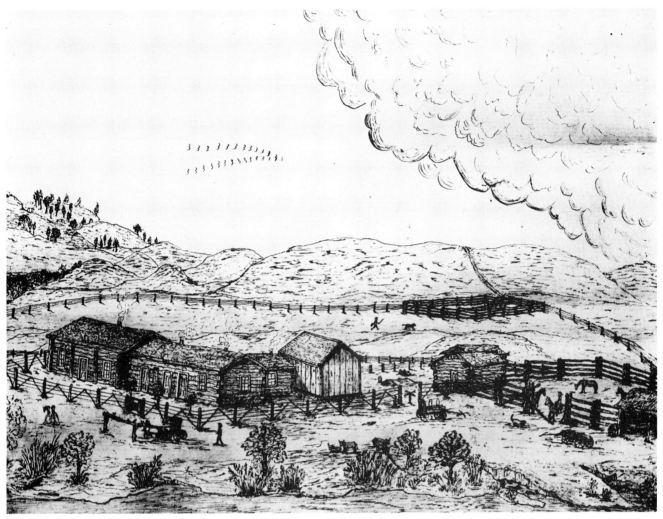

One of Nebraska's first large cattle spreads was the Newman Ranch along the Niobrara River in Sheridan County.

E. S. Newman

The largest spread in Nebraska before 1900 was
put together by Bartlett Richards and William
G. Comstock. Their holdings embraced the
Spade, Bar C, and Overton ranches comprising
more than a half million acres in Cherry, Sheridan, and Box Butte counties. Cattlemen in those
days ran their herds on public lands on which
they paid neither rent nor taxes. Supposedly
these lands were open to homesteaders, but for a
time the big ranchers were able to keep out the
"nesters," as they were called. However, as more
and more homesteaders began taking up their
quarter-sections in the range country and fencing
their land, a conflict was inevitable. Shown above
are Spade cattle being loaded at Ellsworth.

Bartlett Richards

The real cowboys, less photogenic than the television breed, were a flea-bitten, hard-riding, hard-bottomed lot. These Nebraska cowpunchers are shown at dinner (above) during the fall roundup in northwestern Nebraska, and back at the ranch after the roundup (below).

Responding to a demand from eastern markets, Nebraska cattlemen made noticeable progress in breeding better meat-producing cattle. These belonged to the Brighton Ranch about 1890.

Cattle from various ranches often mingled on the range, and ownership was established by the brand the animal bore. Branding time at the Dumbell Ranch near Hyannis is shown here.

Nourishing grass and plenty of water, indispensable to range cattle, characterize the Sandhills of Nebraska. This is the Lee Brothers ranch near Brownlee in 1900.

As homesteaders continued to encroach on the open range, cowboys, equipped with wire-cutters, cut down their fences, and the nesters retaliated by killing cattle that strayed on their land. The most notorious incident in the cattlemen-homesteader conflict in Nebraska occurred in 1878, in Custer County. A gun battle between two homesteaders, Luther Mitchell and Ami Ketchum, and riders for I. P. Olive, one of the wealthiest ranchers in the state, ended in the death of Olive's brother. Mitchell and Ketchum fled east, but eventually surrendered to the law and were lodged temporarily in the Kearney jail.

Olive, according to the trial records, organized a party to hunt down Mitchell and Ketchum when they were returned to Custer County to stand trial.

At Plum Creek, the Olive party was waiting with wagons when the train carrying Mitchell and Ketchum pulled in, and succeeded in taking them prisoner.

At Devil's Gap, near Callaway, Mitchell and Ketchum were hanged (above) and their bodies burned (below).

Olive was found guilty of murder in the second degree, but was discharged on a technicality in 1880. He then removed to Texas, but later turned up in Trail City, Colorado, where he was killed in a saloon fight in August, 1886.

Editor's Note: The photographs on the opposite page and the hanging scene above were re-enacted by volunteers for Solomon D. Butcher, Custer County photographer. The events were photographed in the exact locales of the tragedy.

Nebraska had its share of outlaws and gunmen, but most of them were just traveling through—heading north or west. Among those who stayed were David C. (Doc) Middleton and his gang. Doc specialized in horse stealing, although he did do some cattle rustling. A soft-spoken man and something of a Robin Hood, he frequently gave stolen livestock to homesteaders or small ranchers, and they in gratitude would offer him sanctuary when the law-enforcement officers were too close on his heels. In 1879, he was caught and sentenced to five years for horse stealing. Paroled after three and a half years, Doc went straight, at one time becoming deputy sheriff in Sheridan County. He died ignominiously in 1913, while being held in the county jail of Douglas, Wyoming, for bootlegging. Middleton is shown above. At the right is his famous underground corral and home for his gang, located on the Niobrara River in Holt County.

The Indians: Their Tragedy

By 1872, four years after the Fort Laramie treaty, the Sioux bands led by Red Cloud and Spotted Tail had been located on reservations on the White River in northwestern Nebraska, but the non-treaty Sioux, led by Crazy Horse and Sitting Bull, were still dissaffected and still roaming their former ranges. In 1874 gold was reported in the Black Hills, and although the Hills were part of the lands guaranteed to the Sioux by treaty, there was insistent and increasing agitation to take over the region. For a time the Army did try rather half-heartedly to keep the whites out of Indian country, but when the government was unable to persuade the Sioux to either lease or sell their sacred hunting grounds to the United States, the troops were withdrawn and the prospectors streamed in. In December, 1875, the government sent word to the roving Sioux bands that if they had not come in to their respective reservations by January 31, 1876, they would be considered hostiles. When Crazy Horse, Sitting Bull, and the other chiefs refused to comply, the War Department mounted a campaign to disarm and dismount the recalcitrants.

While the outcome was never in doubt, the Sioux War of 1876 provided some rude jolts to white complacency. General George Crook's forces were turned back at the Rosebud on June 17, and little more than a week later, on June 25, Custer's command was wiped out at the Little Big Horn. But a war cannot be fought without reserves of manpower, arms, and supplies. In February, 1877, Sitting Bull fled to Canada, and in May, Crazy Horse and his remaining followers surrendered their arms. A year later the Sioux reservations in Nebraska were moved across the border to South Dakota.

The Sioux War crushed Indian resistance on the northern plains, but there was to be a tragic epilogue. In 1890, an Indian scare was touched off when the ghost dance, a ritualistic worship of the Indian prophet Wovoka, spread through the reservations. The military was called in, and a combination of panic and blundering on the white man's part led to the massacre of a band of Sioux who were on their way to the agency to surrender. At this "battle," which took place at Wounded Knee Creek a few miles north of the Nebraska border, 44 women, 18 children, and 84 warriors were killed. Many others later died of wounds and exposure.

Between 1870 and 1885 commercial hunters after hides and sportsmen after amusement killed more than ten million buffalo, almost extinguishing the species. The carcasses of the great beasts were left to rot on the prairie. In the late 1880's bone-pickers made a living collecting and selling the bones, which were used in the manufacture of phosphates and carbon.

The buffalo slaughter, which cleared the Plains for the white man's cattle, wiped out the Indian's chief food supply. The next step was to get the Indians onto reservations. Some of the Oglala Sioux were located at the Red Cloud Agency, shown as it appeared in 1876.

Trouble with the Indians seemed inevitable so long as Crazy Horse, Spotted Tail, and other young chiefs refused to accept reservation status. Frederic Remington's famous painting "Twenty-Five to One" depicts one of the frequent clashes between cavalry patrols and the hostiles.

Bolstering its defenses in northwestern Nebraska, in 1874 the Army established Fort Robinson (below) near the Red Cloud Agency.

In the same year, at the urgent request of the Loup Valley settlers, Fort Hartsuff was established on the Loup River.

Even after Crazy Horse had surrendered wi 2,000 of his warriors (left), there were rum that he was going on the warpath. Suspected fomenting a rebellion, he was fatally wound when resisting arrest and died at Fort Robins September 5, 1877. His funeral procession shown (below) passing through Camp Sherid a temporary military post at the Spotted T Agency.

A heroic episode of the Indian resistance occurred when a small band of Cheyennes led by Dull Knife fled from the Oklahoma reservation where they had been placed, and attempted to make their way back to their Montana hunting grounds. In October, 1878, they were captured and confined at Fort Robinson. In the scene above, Dull Knife cries out: "Tell him [the Commandant] if he tries to send us back, we will butcher each other with our own knives." The Cheyennes escaped on January 9, but eventually most were killed or recaptured.

The ghost-dance ritual, which threw the frontier into a panic in 1890, expressed the Indian's hope that the white man would be driven forever from his lands and that the Great Father would restore the buffalo herds. This is the only photograph ever made of the ghost dance.

Sitting Bull, who had returned from Canada in 1881, was killed in a scuffle at the Standing Rock Agency in 1890, and news of his death contributed to the settlers' alarm. In this atmosphere of tension, a band of Sioux was senselessly massacred by the Army at Wounded Knee Creek on December 29, 1890. The bodies were stacked in a common grave for burial.

Rails and Roads

During the period from 1870 to the mid-1890's the railroads played their most important part in the making of the state. Their immigration agencies helped to colonize it; the extension of their lines opened new areas to settlement; their freight trains carried cattle and produce to market. When the first permanent railroad bridge across the Missouri to Omaha was completed in 1872, the Union Pacific made connections with three eastern lines: the Mississippi and Missouri (now the Rock Island), the Chicago, Iowa and Nebraska (now the Chicago and North Western), and the Burlington (which already had begun building west from Plattsmouth). By 1900, when railroad mileage in Nebraska totaled 5,685, the U.P. had double-track lines across the state, and part of the Burlington also was double track. Together with the Fremont, Elkhorn and Missouri Valley (now the North Western) running from Omaha into the northwestern corner of the state, these were the arteries from which the branch lines sprouted.

Local transportation still depended on horse-drawn vehicles. This was the heyday of the "democrat" wagon, with two or more seats; the highly polished black family carriage, with its kerosene lamps; the surrey, with or without the fringe on top; and—most commonly seen of all—the one-horse buggy. For hauling and delivering goods, there were all manner of vans and wagons, including the top-heavy white mail wagons which served the R.F.D. routes. Brick and cedar-block pavements could be found in cities and towns, but beyond the city limits, roads were still mainly deep tracks across the prairie.

The waiting room of the Union Pacific depot in Omaha in 1877. The Black Hills gold rush, which reached its peak in that year, greatly augmented the traffic westward.

Railroading had peculiar perils in Nebraska in the 1870's. Occasionally a train would be held up for more than an hour while a herd of buffalo crossed the tracks. When the Rocky Mountain locusts descended on Nebraska, piles of the insects had to be shoveled off the tracks, which had become so oily and greasy that the locomotive wheels lost traction.

In 1888, a flash flood on Rope Creek near Orleans weakened a bridge, causing the wreck of a Burlington passenger train.

This is the famous 4-4-0 locomotive, workhorse of early railroading in Nebraska. It is shown here at the Waterloo station.

During the Black Hills gold rush, Sidney, on the Union Pacific line, became an outfitting point for prospectors bound for the Hills. It is estimated that as many as 1,500 people passed through the town daily. Supplies were transported overland to the mining camps on freighting trains such as this one, shown pulling out of Sidney.

Road ranches, a precursor of the motel, offered travelers food, drink, and supplies. This is the McDonald Ranch, near Cottonwood Springs, in the 1880's.

The Populists

Everything was coming up roses in the 1880's, but despite boom days the farmer's economic position was steadily worsening. The more he grew, the less he got for his labor and the deeper he went into debt. The problem, as the farmer saw it, was not overproduction but unjustly high freight rates and monopolistic grain elevator practices; it cost him a bushel of grain for every bushel he marketed. He had to borrow money to pay for farm implements and commercial goods, and in bad years—such as the drouth years of the 1890's—many a farmer who had struggled to improve his farm home was foreclosed for debt.

The agrarian protest found a voice in the Farmers' Alliance, from which grew the People's Party, also known as the Populists. Organized nationally in 1891–1892, the party favored free and unlimited coinage of silver at a ratio of 16 to 1, government ownership and operation of transportation and communication lines, direct election of U.S. senators, and the secret ballot. In Nebraska, the "Pops" scored successes in 1890, but the momentum did not carry over into the 1892 election; in 1893, however, the beginning of a long and severe drouth and the nationwide depression brought new adherents to the party. More importantly, a brilliant young congressman from Lincoln, William Jennings Bryan, who took over Democratic leadership in 1894, saw that the Populists and Democrats must unite to become an effective political force. The fusion of the two parties, which Bryan masterminded, enabled the Populists to elect their entire state ticket that year; and in 1896 the fusionists again won all state offices, control of the legislature, and four of the six congressional seats. While the legislature passed a broad range of reform measures, it failed to deal with the railroad problem.

As the drouth years ended and business began to recover, the urgent sense of protest faded away and Populist influence waned. But the farm revolt left a permanent mark on national political thinking, and in the person of William Jennings Bryan it added a new hero to the American pantheon.

The grumbling over low prices during the bountiful 1880's became organized political protest in the 1890 campaign. This is the convention of the Independent People's Party at Columbus in July. In the election that fall, the Populists and Democrats won control of both legislative houses, the governorship, and all three congressional seats.

Elected to Congress on the Democratic ticket in 1890 and 1892, William Jennings Bryan was defeated for senator in 1894. But at the Democratic convention in Chicago in 1896, his dramatic "Cross of Gold" speech, calling for the free and unlimited coinage of silver, won him the presidential nomination.

After the official notification of his nomination at ceremonies on the state capitol grounds in Lincoln (above), Bryan embarked on a fourteen-week campaign during which he made six hundred speeches in twenty-nine states. He is seen below at Stromsburg. Nebraska voted Democrat for the first time in its history, but McKinley won by 600,000 votes.

Twice again—in 1900 and 1908—Bryan was the Democratic nominee for the presidency. Though he failed to be elected, the Great Commoner was an authentic spellbinder, as witness these photographs showing him addressing whistle-stop crowds, and the ideas he voiced so eloquently profoundly influenced the Democrat party and were reflected in "Progressive Republicanism."

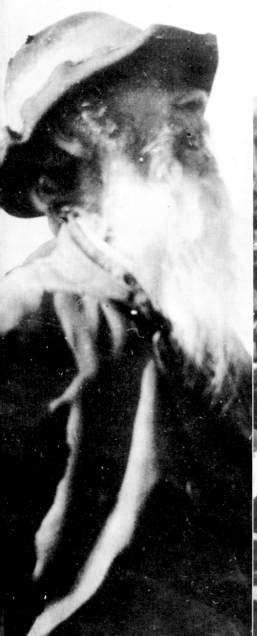

The Spanish-American War

On February 15, 1898, the U.S. battleship *Maine* was blown up in Havana harbor with a loss of 260 lives, and "Remember the *Maine!*" was the rallying cry the following April when the nation's young men, among them, 4,650 Nebraskans, marched off to America's first international war in fifty years. Victory came quickly and—by modern standards—the price was not high: only 379 men were killed in battle although more than 5,000 died of disease and other causes. By the terms of the peace treaty signed in December, Cuba attained her independence from Spain, and Puerto Rico and Guam came to the United States. In addition, Spain ceded the Philippine Islands to the U.S. for twenty million dollars. Philippine insurrectionists led by Emilio Aguinaldo had expected immediate independence, and rose in revolt against the new government when they learned the terms of the treaty. Many Nebraskans who had volunteered to fight Spain instead did their fighting against the Filipino rebels. Although organized resistance had been suppressed by the end of 1899 and Aguinaldo was captured in March, 1901, guerrilla warfare continued until mid-1902.

Company G of the 2nd Nebraska Regiment is shown training at Camp George H. Thomas in Georgia. Below is Camp Santa Mesa, just east of Manila, P.I., as it appeared in January, 1899. It included the bivouac of the 1st Nebraska Regiment.

Here is the 1st Nebraska (above) as it paraded up Farnam Street in Omaha upon its return from the Philippines in the summer of 1899. In September, the regiment returned its battle-scarred flags at a ceremony on the statehouse grounds in Lincoln (below).

Main Street

During the great boom of the 1880's, traditionally conservative Nebraska temporarily stepped out of character and went on a speculative binge. As James C. Olson has written: "Progress was in the air. The good crops, the railroads, the growing population all suggested great things. Any town could become a commercial center or a great railway metropolis, or both. . . . Not a few believed that in time the greatness of the new West would necessitate the abandonment of Washington for a national headquarters on the Plains. Raw villages indulged in rosy dreams of greatness, and gas lights twinkled where the coyotes should have been left undisturbed. Everywhere the dreams of greatness were implemented with borrowed money . . . ." During the decade, Omaha's population, 30,000 in 1880, nearly quadrupled, stimulated by the phenomenal growth of its packing plants and other industries. In Lincoln, enthusiasts prophesied that its population of 40,000 in 1885 would reach 100,000 in 1890. Beatrice, Kearney, Hastings, Grand Island, Fremont, and Norfolk were caught up in the excitement and went all out to attract new industry and population.

The hard times of the 1890's brought the state back to reality with a resounding bump. Nevertheless, impressive gains had been registered and by the turn of the century, as the state recovered from the depression and the drouth ended, local promoters were again beating the drum, although not quite so hard. But despite the population trend toward the cities, Nebraska still remained predominantly an agricultural state, a state of small towns and villages. For most Nebraskans at this time, town life meant not O Street or Farnam, but Main Street. Main Street, by whatever name it was called, characteristically boasted a post office, livery barns, general stores, drug stores, an implement dealer's, a bank, and—vexing though it was to a good part of the female population and the temperance societies—a saloon.

The corner of Fifth and Market Streets in
Beatrice, 1887.

Kearney on a busy Saturday afternoon in 1898.

Main Street, Wausa, in 1894.

Lincoln, at Eleventh and P Streets, in 1889. At the end of the street stands University Hall, which opened its doors in September, 1871, two years after the University of Nebraska had been chartered by the legislature.

Lincoln in 1892, celebrating the twenty-fifth anniversary of its founding. The large building at the left was the city's new post office.

Omaha's Farnam Street in 1889.

The lion's share of industry in Nebraska during the 1880's and 1890's was located in Omaha. By far the largest employers were the meat packers. This is the Cudahy plant in South Omaha in 1896.

Industries related to agriculture dotted Nebraska. Chief among them were the grain mills whose wheels were turned by water power. This mill was on the Niobrara River east of Valentine.

Retail trade was the lifeblood of business in Nebraska's many small towns. The blacksmith and wagon shop, like the one above in Broken Bow, and the general store—Beaver City's is shown below—were fixtures in any thriving community in the 1890's.

Conceived by Omaha businessmen during the depth of the depression in 1895, the Trans-Mississippi and International Exhibition, which opened its doors on June 1, 1898, was a brilliantly effective demonstration that prosperity had returned and Nebraska was moving ahead. Forty states and ten nations had exhibits at the fair. Cass Gilbert designed the pavilion devoted to agriculture; and the famed hootchy-kootchy dancer Little Egypt was the prime attraction on the midway. The war with Spain had begun only a few days before the fair opened, but nonetheless it was a smashing success; and before it closed in November even President McKinley had come to Omaha to view the spectacle.

The End of the Frontier

The official date for the end of the frontiering period is 1890, the year in which the United States Census Director announced in his report that "there can hardly be said to be a frontier line." There was still some pioneering to be done in Nebraska, but certainly by the turn of the century the most dramatic aspects of Nebraska's robust frontier life belonged to the past. The Indian scouts, the dashing cavalrymen, the stagecoach drivers and bullwhackers, the outlaws and the shoot-from-the-hip peace officers still thronged the pages of popular fiction, but their real-life prototypes—Frank and Luther North, Wild Bill Hickok, Doc Middleton, Kid Wade, and many others who drifted in and out of the state—had long since been stretched out or retired. William F. Cody, however, sensed the enormous appeal of this phase of American history and planned a Wild West show that would, as his sister wrote, "delineate in throbbing and realistic color . . . the wigwam village; the Indian war-dance; the life of scouts and trappers; the hunting of the buffalo; the slow, perilous progress of the settlers in the prairie schooners over the vast and desolate plains; the Deadwood stage and the Pony Express; the making of homes in the face of fire and Indian massacre; the United States cavalry and 'Death to the Sioux!' . . ." Cody's show prospered mightily, and from that day to our own the heroes and villains of the Old West have lived again in the various entertainment media. The frontier had ended in Nebraska, but the legend would survive.

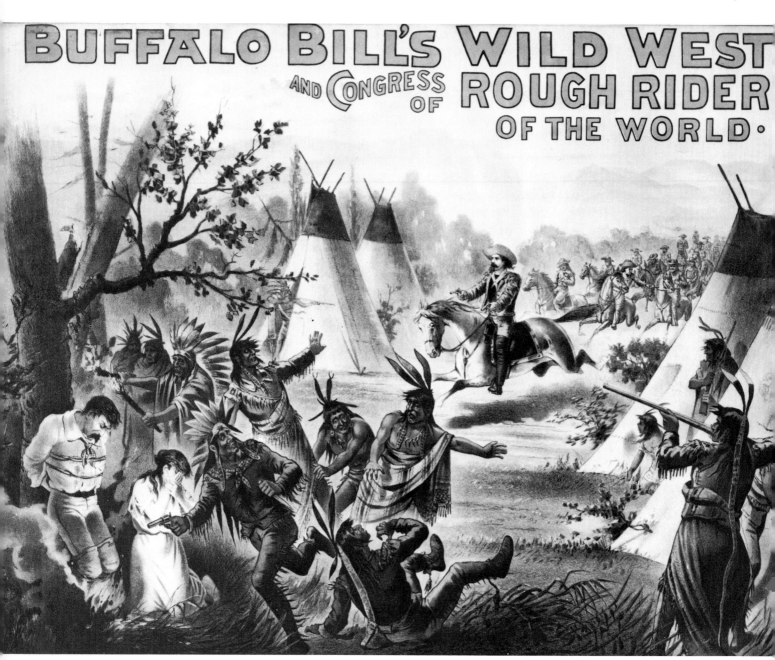

It was good, clean, exciting fun—the frontier wrapped in one rousing, glamorous package—and posters like this brought customers flocking to Buffalo Bill's Wild West Show. First presented in Omaha in May, 1883, the show eventually played in nearly every city on the civilized globe.

Here is the Cody troup, complete with Indians
and the famous old Indian scout Johnny Nelson
atop the Deadwood stagecoach, ready for the
grand entrance when the show played at the
World's Columbian Exposition—better known as
the Chicago World's Fair—in 1893.

At Scout's Rest Ranch, his home in North Platte, Colonel Cody played host to theatrical road companies as well as all manner of visiting firemen. Here is the Boston Opera Company, touring in *The Bohemian Girl*, stopped off for a brief taste of the frontier.

The Great Thousand Mile Horse Race from Chadron to the entrance of Buffalo Bill's Wild West Show at the Chicago Fair was run in June, 1893. The first to reach the goal was John Berry, who completed the ride in thirteen days and sixteen hours, but apparently he and his mount had made part of the trip in a freight car—at any rate, he didn't collect the prize. One of the competitors was Doc Middleton, Nebraska's reformed gentleman outlaw—that's Doc with the flowing beard, in the left center of the picture.

THE GOOD OLD DAYS
(1900-1930)

For every generation there is a period in the not-too-remote past that is thought of with special nostalgia as "the good old days"—a period when life appears to have been more colorful and more spacious, perhaps richer and certainly easier than the present. Regardless of the ups and downs the history books show, and no matter what headaches and crises and catastrophes were blazoned in the headlines, to Nebraskans in the mid-1960's the first three decades of the twentieth century seem largely compounded of halcyon days; even the First World War, in comparison with what we have since experienced, seems almost a romantic adventure.

The 1900–1930 period was blessed for the most part with adequate rainfall and bountiful crops. Much of the backbreaking toil of farming, done by man and horse in the nineteenth century, was now increasingly accomplished with the help of a remarkable series of innovations in farm machinery powered by the gasoline-driven tractor. New crop varieties, new tilling practices, and improved livestock breeding resulted in greater productivity and superior quality. The automobile and the truck put an end to the traditional isolation of the farmer and rancher, and offered to all Nebraskans the advantages and adventures of mobility. Electricity, coal and gas, the telephone and the radio, as they became common commodities and services, contributed to the general well-being.

Of course, not all groups were uniformly prosperous at any one time. In 1914, for example, when, according to one historian, Nebraska ranked first in per capita wealth, second in per capita automobile ownership, and had the smallest percentage of illiteracy of any state, the Kinkaiders in northwestern Nebraska were finding life as hard as it had been for the pioneers in the '70's. And during the golden years of the 1920's, the decline of crop prices caused many farm foreclosures and bank failures. Still, as we look back, the temper of the times except for the war years seems even enough, and the problems minor. Once the war was won, the focus was on domestic matters—crop surpluses, better roads for the tin lizzies, prohibition and the ensuing gang warfare, the movies, sporting events, and the changes in morals and manners symbolized by bobbed hair, short skirts, hip flasks, and the Charleston. International conferences, in the good old days, were largely concerned with disarmament—and *moon* was a word that rhymed with *June*.

Down on the Farm

The tractor and the implements it pulled or powered reshaped Nebraska agriculture between 1900 and 1930. While the tractor required a greater initial investment, it enabled the farmer eventually to dispense with nearly 250,000 horses and mules and the substantial acreage of forage crops needed to feed them; it permitted him to care for more acres and accelerated the trend toward larger farms; and it reduced the man-hours of labor. During this period, too, irrigation became an integral part of farming in the upper North Platte Valley. The long-sought satisfactory cash crop was found in winter wheat varieties developed from the old Turkey Red variety by the University of Nebraska College of Agriculture. The dairy industry expanded rapidly and the beef cattle industry continued to grow.

Viewing Nebraska in a 1923 article, Willa Cather wrote of the changing rural scene and way of life. "The old isolated farms have come together," she said. "The whole state is a farm. Now it is the pasture lands that look little and lonely, crowded in among so much wheat and corn. It is scarcely an exaggeration to say that every farmer owns an automobile. . . . The great grain fields are plowed by tractors. The old farmhouses are rapidly being replaced by more cheerful dwellings, with bathrooms and hardwood floors, heated by furnaces or hot-water plants. Many of them are lighted by electricity and every farmhouse has a telephone. The country towns are clean and well kept. On Saturday night the main street is a long, black line of parked motor cars; the farmers have brought their families to see the motion-picture show. When the school bell rings on Monday morning, crowds of happy looking children, well-nourished—for the most part well mannered, too—flock along the shady streets. They wear cheerful, modern clothes, and the girls, like the boys, are elastic and vigorous in their movements. These thousands and thousands of children—in the little towns and in the country schools—these, of course, ten years from now will be the state."

Plumes of black smoke hung over the landscape as the steam thresher moved from field to field. This thresher was at work in Kearney County in 1910.

Gang plows, drawn by this huge iron-wheel tractor, greatly expedited the task of turning the Nebraska sod. This scene is in Buffalo County in the early 1900's.

Petroleum-fueled tractors were introduced in the state in the early 1900's. It was this combined harvest operation, photographed near Ogallala in 1918, which helped Nebraska produce the food required for victory in World War I.

The combined threshing-and-harvesting operation was further refined in this model of the 1920's, shown at work in Red Willow County.

Some farmers stayed with horsepower and the reaper-binder. This familiar pastoral scene, so long associated with farming, was photographed in Lancaster County in the early 1920's.

Because of the demand for grain and spiraling prices, thousands of acres of prairie in western Nebraska were plowed up during the World War I years. Here is a 1925 view of the big-wheat country in the Imperial Valley of Chase County.

The state's efforts at irrigation were negligible until the passage of the Federal Reclamation Act of 1902. During the next twenty-five years about 150,000 acres of arid land in Morrill and Scotts Bluff counties were brought under irrigation. This is the conversion dam as it looked in 1930, channeling the life-giving water north and south of the North Platte River.

With irrigation, intensive farming came to the upper North Platte River. This 1926 photograph shows a potato field.

Irrigation also brought sugar beets, beet-sugar factories, and a booming cattle-feeding enterprise to the Scotts Bluff area, as shown above in 1927.

With the growth of towns during the first third of the century, the task of supplying their residents with dairy products became specialized.

The old dual-purpose red cow was supplanted by quality herds like this one, shown soaking up the noonday sun.

This was considered a model dairy farm in the mid-1920's. It was located in Red Willow County.

Milk-processing plants, operating with improved machinery and sanitation standards, exported their products to eastern markets as well as supplying Nebraska. The creamery shown here was in Orleans.

Cattlemen continued to improve their breeds and cattle prices remained steady during the long agricultural decline of the 1920's. This herd of white faces was photographed in Cherry County in the early '20's.

In pioneer days, the farmer's wife might not hear another woman's voice for weeks at a time. The telephone (right) changed this situation. Not only was it a great boon in emergencies but it provided her with a new recreation, particularly if she was on a party line. Coal-burning stoves (below), electric lights, and washing machines went a long way to ease her burden.

The last land frontier in the state was opened to settlement by the Kinkaid Act of 1904, which affected thirty-seven western Nebraska counties. Patents were authorized on tracts up to 640 acres after five years of residence and proof of improvements to the value of $1.25 per acre. Even with this increased acreage, however, the Kinkaiders found the going rugged. The photograph above, taken in Cherry County in 1926, shows a Kinkaider's house with its wall made of baled hay.

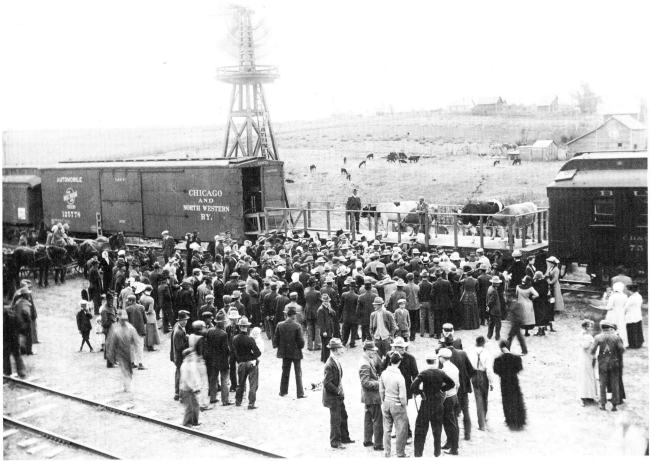

To help farmers adjust to the changes in agriculture, the cooperative agricultural extension service program was initiated at the University of Nebraska in 1914. Shown at Farnum in the early 1920's is an extension "Dairy Special," sent out by arrangement with the Union Pacific and Burlington railroads.

Wheels and Wings

Our urge to get from here to there faster was substantially appeased in the first three decades of the twentieth century. The first horseless carriage was seen in Nebraska before 1900, and in 1906 there were more than a thousand in the state. At first, the automobile was regarded as a curiosity; later, as a noisy, horse-frightening nuisance; all the same, by 1910 some 15,000 motor cars were bouncing over section-line roads and city streets. Then in 1914, Henry Ford revolutionized the automotive industry with his assembly-line processes, and with the advent of the tin lizzie, the automobile ceased to be a rich man's toy.

As more and more people became car owners, the demand for better roads increased proportionately, but it was soon apparent that the state could not cope with the problem. The answer was the federal aid road program to develop the nation's highway system. Initiated in 1916, it operated on a basis of matching funds. By 1930, about 15 per cent of the total designated road system of the state had been improved, with 310 miles paved, 5,000 miles graveled, and 3,300 miles graded.

Heavier-than-air flying machines were first seen in Nebraska skies a half-dozen years after the successful flight of the Wright Brothers at Kitty Hawk, in 1903. Many a Nebraskan made his first flight in the years following World War I, when barnstorming pilots appeared at fairs and took up anyone who had five dollars and the necessary nerve. During the 1920's some aircraft were built in the state and flying schools multiplied. By 1930, air mail and air passenger service were a part of Nebraska life. But most long-distance travel still was by car or train, and the railroads responded to the accelerated tempo of the times by developing steam locomotives which could pull passenger trains at speeds up to a hundred miles an hour and hundred-car freight trains at a mile a minute.

Something new appeared on Main Street in the early part of the twentieth century—the auto livery, later to be known as the garage. This one was in Merna in 1910.

There was nothing like seeing what the automobile could do, either full speed ahead on the level or assaulting a steep bank, as demonstrated by this gentleman from Kearney in 1911.

Roads in pre-World War I days were, in a word, terrible. When it rained you could count on sinking into mud up to the hubcaps—or even deeper if you happened to hit a dip in the road. It was said that a farmer with a sturdy team of horses could make more money pulling motorists out of the mud than he could farming.

After 1916, graveled "all-weather" roads built
with federal aid began to appear on road maps.
Shown above is work being done on the Fremont-
Ceresco highway. The first hard-surfaced stretch
of road built in Nebraska with federal help ran
from Lincoln to Emerald.

The cross-country motorist in the good old days also had to be a pathfinder. Before 1930, routes were seldom marked, except perhaps with a few stripes on telephone poles. If you wanted to know where the road led, you stopped and asked a farmer.

Cities now had to deal with the new problem of traffic control. The first attempt to solve it took the form of a human "stop signal"—the traffic cop planted in the middle of a busy intersection. This scene is in Lincoln in the early 1920's.

The airplane first appeared in the Nebraska skies in the first decade of the century. Here is the first one flown at Kearney. The year is 1911. It is not known whether the lady at the controls really intended to leave the ground.

Barnstorming pilots, many of them World War I
flyers, thrilled Nebraskans at fairs and air shows.
This 1927 exhibition ended disastrously in a
grove of trees near Omaha.

Charles A. Lindbergh, who attended a Lincoln flying school in 1922, is shown here on a goodwill visit to Omaha in 1928. The plane is the "Spirit of St. Louis," in which the Lone Eagle had made the first nonstop solo flight across the Atlantic the year before.

When transcontinental air mail service began in 1921, the historic Platte Valley route was followed across Nebraska. Here is a Boeing plane being loaded at the Omaha airport in 1929.

Regular air passenger service became a feature of
Nebraska life in the '20's, but its appeal initially
was for the adventurous. This 1930 photograph
shows a Ford tri-motor transport at the Omaha
airport.

The golden age of railroad passenger service came between 1900 and 1930. In 1916, railroad mileage in Nebraska peaked at 8,332 miles. This is the Burlington station in Lincoln in 1910.

By 1910, five major railroad companies were operating in the state. The Rock Island's Eastbound No. 6 train is shown in this 1912 photograph as it arrives at Fairbury.

Steam locomotives were continually improved. The Burlington's Hudson type, developed for fast passenger service, is seen here pulling the Burlington's crack "Aristocrat."

Over There!

When a general European war broke out in August, 1914, the nation's initial reaction was that we should keep out of it, and this was an attitude that persisted in the Midwest almost up to April 6, 1917, when war was declared against Germany. Nebraska, like many of the heartland states, was a crucible for all the nationalistic animosities of the Old World, a majority of its citizens having blood ties with most of the combatant nations. Public sentiment was predominantly pro-Ally, but the largest single ethnic group in the state was of German origin. Many of the most influential members of this group believed that the Fatherland's cause was just, and the German case was stated in some forty German-language newspapers, as well as from church pulpits. Moreover, many believed with William Jennings Bryan that American neutrality was essential to the nation's best interest. In 1915, Bryan, who was Secretary of State in the Wilson Cabinet, resigned his post when he felt the President was becoming overinvolved with the Allies. Similarly, Senator George W. Norris fought bitterly to preserve American neutrality and voted against America's entry into the war.

Despite Wilson's campaign slogan—"He kept us out of war!"—which helped to re-elect him, it was increasingly apparent that this country would be drawn into the conflict. Early in 1917, as war with Germany became imminent, the President recalled troops which had been serving on a punitive expedition in Mexico. A contingent of the Nebraska National Guard had been among those stationed along the Mexican border.

During the eighteen months of U.S. participation in World War I, Nebraska sent 57,526 men and women into the armed forces; of these 1,655 were killed or wounded. On the home front Nebraska had a balloon school at Fort Omaha and a cavalry training center at Fort Robinson.

After America was committed to fight, the war of words in Nebraska gave way to violence and hysteria. Books written in German were burned, the teaching of German was forbidden, and it was considered unpatriotic to play the music of German composers. Yellow paint was splashed on the houses of so-called slackers, and white feathers handed to young men who were not in uniform. Several University of Nebraska faculty members were accused of failing to support the war effort, and two were asked to resign after a public hearing. While fighting to make the world safe for democracy, Nebraskans nearly lost it at home.

I WANT YOU
FOR U.S. ARMY
NEAREST RECRUITING STATION

World War I saw the first systematic use of propaganda to mobilize the nation for the war effort. Prior to our entrance into the war there had been "Preparedness" parades, then came a barrage of posters and Liberty Loan drives. The posters, which were surprisingly effective, took a variety of forms. There was the direct appeal, exemplified by the James Montgomery Flagg poster (above), which was used again in World War II, and the portrayal of the German as a barbaric Hun (right). Others proclaiming "Food Will Win the War!" and "The Navy Needs You! Don't Read American History—Make It!" could be seen in every Nebraska community.

REMEMBER ·BELGIUM·
Buy Bonds
Fourth
Liberty
Loan

In September, 1916, the Nebraska National Guard was ordered to Camp Deming, New Mexico, for duty on the Mexican border. Shown above, Company A of the 5th Regiment marches down O Street to the Lincoln station. The soldier saying good-bye below clearly believes that modesty is the best policy.

Many Nebraska recruits took their basic training at Camp Funston, in Kansas. Shown above doing calisthenics are members of the 355th Infantry Regiment. Back in Nebraska, the Home Guard units practiced close-order drill. The unit below is at Ravenna.

A Red Cross sale at Wahoo (above) on July 4, 1918, resumes after a passing shower had left the street a sea of mud.

General John J. Pershing, who was named Commander-in-Chief of the American Expeditionary Forces in May, 1917, had been Commandant of the University of Nebraska Cadet Corps (1891–1895) and received an LL.B. degree from the University in 1893. He is seen here with Secretary of War Newton D. Baker inspecting a 155mm gun at Bordeaux, France, in March, 1918.

On November 11, 1918, it was all over, over here, and before long our boys were on their way home. Here is the *Leviathan* docking in New York harbor with a major contingent of Nebraskans aboard. The welcoming committee is shown at the left.

Principal war industries in Nebraska were potash plants located in lake areas of the Sandhills. Little Antioch was transformed into a town of 2,500 as five factories in the area operated around the clock. When the war ended, the factories closed and the buildings deteriorated into rusting skeletons.

On and Off Main Street

In retrospect, the first fifteen years of the twentieth century seems an idyllic period, a sort of age of innocence. The social ferment of the Populist period had subsided now that the farmer enjoyed relatively good crops and prices. Towns grew steadily as the population drift from the farm continued. Life was more comfortable for everybody, and there was more time to enjoy it. In summer, on Sundays and holidays you could count on a band concert; the banjo and the mandolin enlivened picnics, and every town had a baseball team. In winter there were taffy pulls and skating parties and sleighing. Chautauqua and church socials entertained and inspired, and there were still many touring theatrical companies, although by 1915 local opera houses already were being converted into movie theaters, and everyone knew "Our Mary," Douglas Fairbanks, Charlie Chaplin, William S. Hart, and other early stars of the silver screen.

After World War I, however, the picture changed sharply—and some would say not for the better. Votes for women were now a reality, and the Charlestoning flapper, with her bobbed hair and short skirts, became a symbol of the decade that has been called the Jazz Age and the Roaring Twenties. Prohibition, operating in reverse, made drinking a favorite indoor sport and the bootlegger a much sought-after fellow. The headlines were about equally divided between the gangland slayings of Al Capone's mobsters and rival hoodlums and the exploits of sports heroes—Babe Ruth, Red Grange, the Four Horsemen, Bobby Jones, and such women stars as the tennis champion Helen Wills and Gertrude Ederle, conqueror of the English Channel. Radio created many new popular idols—in Nebraska the first interstate broadcasting was done from Hastings, Oak, and David City over Station KFOR. Just about every family had a car, and it became harder and harder to stay home.

At the turn of the century, the Fourth of July celebration was a day-long affair, with a parade, speeches, band concert, athletic contests, and special events such as the balloon ascension (above) at Broken Bow in 1903. Another fixture was the baseball game. The one shown was played at Stratton in 1901.

Life was easy and unhurried, and social gatherings—like this Lincoln picnic—were characterized by the Midwest's own brand of Victorian gentility. For the small fry, the high point of the summer was the day the circus came to town. Below, the Sells-Floto Circus parades before the big show at Kearney in 1908.

In 1908, for the third time William Jennings
Bryan was the Democratic nominee for the presidency, and again was defeated, this time by
William Howard Taft. Bryan is shown here
being notified of his nomination at Fairview, his
home in Lincoln.

The traveling Chautauqua programs, usually held in tents, brought famous speakers and good music to every part of the state. Here is the Chautauqua at Kearney.

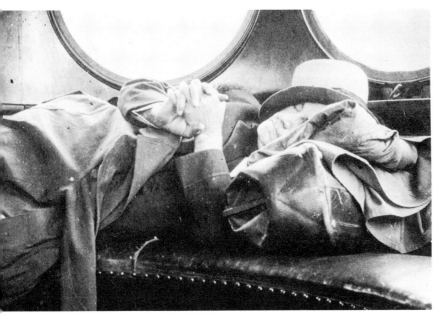

For many years W. J. Bryan was a star attraction on the Chautauqua circuit. Above he is seen napping on the train en route to the next stop on the tour. At right are posters advertising his appearance on the Chautauqua bill.

National recognition that the University of Nebraska had developed into a leading educational institution came in 1909, when it became the eighteenth university chosen for membership in the Association of American Universities. This 1910 photograph shows coeds turned out for a dandelion-digging project.

Main street of the capital city—the Thirteenth and O intersection—all lit up on a cold March night in 1912.

On Easter Sunday, March 23, 1913, a tornado plowed a path a quarter of a mile wide diagonally across Omaha. It killed 140, injured 350, and left 2,500 homeless. Property damage exceeded $1,000,000.

Prohibition had been a lively issue in Nebraska since territorial days. In 1917, Nebraska finally voted dry, and the old-time saloon was no more. This was Ben Kriemer's saloon in Talmage not long before his doors were closed.

The influenza epidemic of 1918 claimed many lives. This postman is wearing a mask, hoping to avoid catching the bug.

With the war ended and the boys back home, community life returned to normal. This is Albion on a warm August afternoon in 1919.

The University of Nebraska football team, long an object of admiration to Cornhusker citizens, vaulted into national prominence in the 1920's. This 1922 game, played on old Nebraska Field, helped out. The score: Nebraska: 14, Notre Dame: 6.

In the 1920's the radio became standard equipment in Nebraska homes. Above is the powerful transmitter of KFAB when the station was located in Lincoln. Every boy with a spark of inquisitiveness put together his own crystal set.

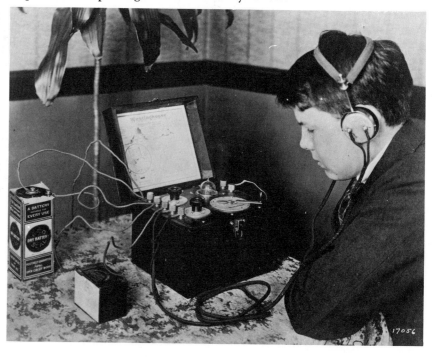

Going to the movies was the prime form of entertainment in the 1920's. Toward the end of the decade, the "talkies" supplanted the old silent films.

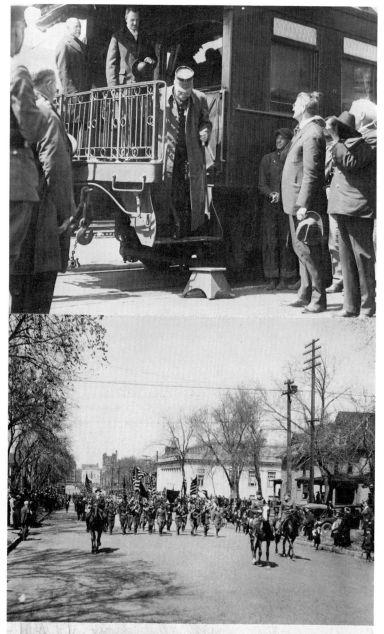

Groundbreaking ceremonies for Nebraska's new state capitol were held on April 14, 1922. The guest of honor was Field Marshal Joseph J. C. Joffre, commander of the allied armies in France in World War I, shown descending from the train on his arrival in Lincoln.

The parade up Fifteenth Street to the capitol grounds.

Governor Samuel R. McKelvie addresses the crowd before the ground-breaking ritual.

Construction on the capitol had progressed to
this point by September, 1928.

Charles W. Bryan, brother of the Great Commoner and three times elected Nebraska's governor, was nominated for Vice President on the Democratic ticket in 1924. Here is the parade in his honor in July of that year as it proceeds down Lincoln's O Street.

The Ku Klux Klan, a southern institution, moved north in the postwar period and Klaverns were organized from coast to coast. In the mid-1920's the Klan exercised considerable political influence. The Klansmen above were photographed at Neligh in 1926.

The big dance craze of the '20's was the Charleston. The chief of police banned it in Lincoln's public dance halls in 1926.

Bobbed hair became the vogue in the early 1920's. During this decade, too, the ladies agreed that they should "reach for a Lucky instead of a sweet" and public smoking by women gradually ceased to evoke consternation and raised eyebrows.

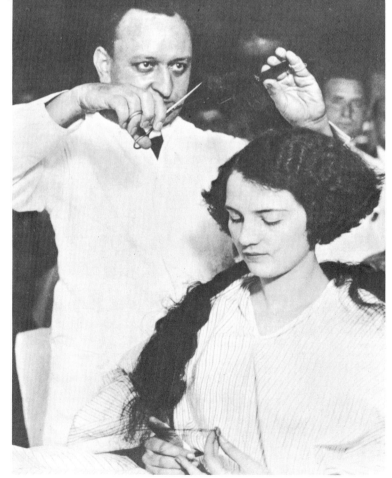

In 1927, Nebraska topped the agricultural states in crop production, so it was no problem to find a first-rate field for the annual cornhusking contest, held that year in Seward County. Note the caps—they were the thing to wear in those days.

While Nebraska's farm production was piling up big surpluses, prices continued to decline—and this in a period of great national prosperity. The situation evoked the comment at right from the Omaha *World-Herald*'s cartoonist.

Here is Omaha's busy Farnam Street in the summer of 1929, as a fabulous period draws to a close. On October 29, the New York stock market crash would usher in America's worst economic crisis. Depression was just around the corner.

CRISES AND RECOVERY
(1930-1955)

The Great Depression of the 1930's is now thirty years in the past, but even in retrospect it looms as a grim and punishing time, which deeply affected the outlook of all who lived through it. After the collapse of the stock market, farm prices plummeted. In 1929, corn sold for 67 cents a bushel; in 1932, it was down to 13 cents. Wheat during the same period dropped from $1.00 to 27 cents; beef cattle from $10.50 to $4.10; hogs from $8.20 to $2.30. The state's economy was keyed to agriculture and many businesses failed. Thousands were out of work and exhausted their savings while fruitlessly looking for jobs. Drouth struck in 1930 and continued throughout the decade. In 1934, only 14.31 inches of rain fell—the driest year since the 1870's. The soil dried up and remorseless winds buried roads, fields, and farmsteads in drifts of dust. For several years, grasshoppers as well as dust clouds blackened the sky. There was genuine fear that much of Nebraska's soil might never recover.

A massive program of federal aid to agriculture, business, and the unemployed began in 1933. Farm foreclosures were halted, but by 1936 more than three hundred Nebraska banks had failed, and by 1937 nearly 100,000 Nebraskans were on relief. Though conditions were somewhat improved as the decade ended, there was to be no appreciable reduction in the expenditures for relief until World War II brought a boom-time economy.

From Pearl Harbor to V-J Day, Nebraskans were one with the nation in an all-out war effort. After victory came, prices continued to climb and in 1947 for the first time Nebraska's farm income exceeded a billion dollars. By then we had learned the hard way better methods of managing our basic resources, soil and water. We also had begun to realize that the federal government, whether we liked it or not, was to play a vastly larger role in our lives.

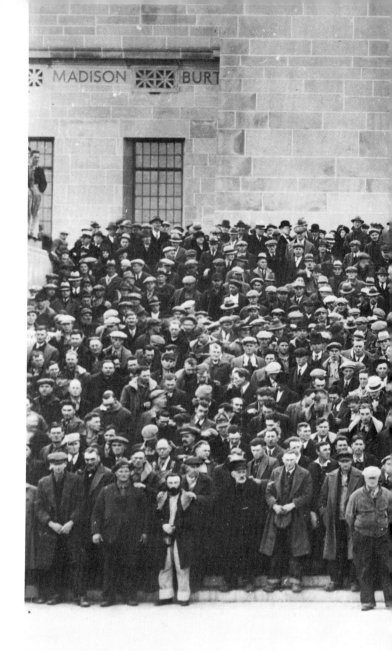

In 1932, as the drouth and depression worsened, Nebraska farmers marched on the state capitol to demand of the legislature a moratorium on farm and home mortgage foreclosures. They got it. In the same year the Farm Holiday Association was organized to withhold farm products from markets until better prices were offered. In the photograph below, striking dairy farmers are picketing a road into Omaha. Trucks bearing milk were overturned if the driver refused to return to the farm.

THE·SALVATION·
OF·THE·STATE·IS·
WATCHFULNESS·
IN·THE·CITIZEN

GAGE ✸ KIMBALL

132

As the anguish and anger of the Nebraska farmers increased, far-left groups in the East saw their chance to move in. One agitator of the American Communist Party was "Mother" Ella Reeve Bloor, 72, shown here. She addressed a rally at Loup City on June 14, 1934, and in what became known as the Loup City Riot, fist fights broke out and the agitators fled. Mother Bloor subsequently served a thirty-day jail sentence for inciting to riot.

In 1934, ten consecutive days of over a hundred degree temperature literally destroyed a promising but shallow-rooted field of corn (left). At right, a field of corn stripped bare by grasshoppers in 1933. Below, burying cattle killed by heat and drouth in Jefferson County in 1936.

Approaching dust storms at Alma (above) and at Naponee (below) in the spring of 1935. When the storms were at full intensity, these communities were in virtual darkness at midday.

Sand drifts resulting from wind erosion near Neligh in 1938 (above). Soil erosion which under-mined the footing caused this farm home in Box Butte County to fall apart in 1937 (below).

An abandoned church in Gage County converted
into a farmhouse in 1938.

A farmer near Arcadia, burned out by the drouth, packs up and heads east for Indiana.

Thousands of farmers and unemployed city dwellers left the state during the dusty 1930's.

Many who stayed in the state were sustained by a wide variety of relief programs, among them

this canning center established in Norfolk in 1934.

When streetcars began to be replaced by buses in Lincoln in 1935, the job of removing the tracks was given to relief workers.

A massive soil-conservation program began in the mid-1930's under federal auspices. Here a terraced field is being contour plowed.

Erosion scarred much farm land, and control measures were begun in every county. The scene above is in Nance County.

Workers of the Civilian Conservation Corps (CCC) terrace land being put back into native grasses in Butler County. Nebraska was one of the first states to be completely organized under state-federal soil-conservation districts.

Nebraskans in the 1930's were in the mood for innovation. In 1934 they approved a one-house nonpartisan legislature, a proposal which found acceptance partly because it was strongly supported by Senator George W. Norris. Members of the first unicameral legislature, which convened in 1937, are shown being sworn in.

A second innovation was the law enacted by the 1933 legislature permitting Nebraskans to organize public power and irrigation districts. Four years later the unicameral legislature authorized organization of the Consumers Public Power District, which subsequently issued bonds and purchased the fourteen private electric power companies in the state at a cost of $40,000,000. Nebraska thus became the only state where all power systems were owned by the public. Shown above is the Loup River Public Power District's plant, which began generating electricity in March, 1937. The Central Nebraska Public Power and Irrigation District (the Tri-County) started generating power from the Kingsley Dam in 1941.

The major innovation in twentieth-century railroad transportation was development of diesel locomotive power by the Burlington. Here is the pioneer Zephyr speeding across a section of Nebraska on its maiden run, May 26, 1934.

The day of the steam locomotive was passing. Many would miss the billowing smoke and wailing steam whistle of such giants as this one, shown on the Union Pacific main line in western Nebraska.

In the severe drouth year of 1935, three days of heavy rainfall in southwest Nebraska caused a Republican River flood which claimed about 100 lives, destroyed 8,000 head of livestock, and damaged 60,000 acres of farm land. Above, a rooftop tossed on the twisted rails of the Burlington main line tracks.

Huge grants of emergency relief funds implemented highway, street, and county road improvement in '30's and early '40's. The Fairmont interchange of Highways 6 and 81 (below) was completed in this period.

After Pearl Harbor, Nebraska focused its energies on the war effort. Army Air Force training bases were located at Alliance, Ainsworth, Bruning (shown above), Fairmont, Grand Island, Harvard, Kearney, Lincoln, McCook, Scottsbluff, and Scribner. Ordnance plants were established at Mead (below right), Grand Island, and Sidney, and a Navy ammunition depot at Hastings. Early in the war citizens joined in gathering scrap to be used in the manufacture of war materials. This junk pile (below left) was collected in West Point. Meanwhile, the rains had returned and, as in World War I, Nebraska's primary contribution to the war effort was foodstuffs.

Of the nearly 140,000 Nebraskans who served in the armed forces during World War II, 3,839 lost their lives. Nebraska's 134th Infantry Regiment played an important role in the battle for Saint-Lô in Normandy, and served with distinction with the Ninth Army on its sweep through Germany. Members of the regiment are shown here in Duer, Germany, preparing to start a house-to-house search.

It's all over! V-J Day in Omaha, August 14, 1945.

Nebraska's universities and colleges were inundated by the flood of ex-GI's. Many of the freshmen were married men with children, like this student with his family at the University of Nebraska.

Building contractors in the immediate postwar years were hard put to keep ahead of the demand for housing. Accelerated by the home-building provision of the GI bill, large housing developments were found in nearly every city and town. This one was in Lincoln.

Even though the rainfall was adequate in the 1940's, Nebraskans had not forgotten the dusty '30's. In 1944, the twin programs of soil and water conservation were given a strong forward thrust when the Congress approved the Missouri Basin Development Program, with its far-reaching provisions for irrigation, flood control, and soil conservation. The program began almost immediately in the Republican River watershed, and by 1949 the Medicine Creek reservoir dam, shown above, had reached this stage of construction. Three other reservoirs were in preliminary stages of construction.

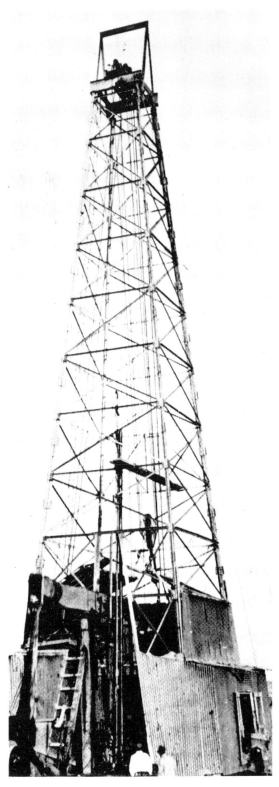

Beginning with the turn of the century, Nebraskans were frequently fast-talked into undertaking oil-drilling ventures, most of which were pure swindles. At long last, on July 27, 1940, the Bucholz Well in Richardson County (left) became the first commercial producer to qualify for the $15,000 bonus offered by the State of

Nebraska. Nine years later came the big oil bonanza, when the Mary Egging No. 1 Well (right) was brought in north of Sidney. Oil of good quality was found in virtually every Panhandle county, and by 1955 Nebraska ranked fourteenth among oil-producing states.

In the decade following the end of World War II, Nebraska weather lived up to its historic reputation for violence. The 1949 blizzard, which swept over the western two-thirds of the state, was one of the worst on record. Shown above, a Burlington snow plow in north central Nebraska. In May, 1953, Hebron was virtually leveled by a tornado. Below is one of the main streets the next morning.

A coal train from Wyoming winds up Crawford Hill in the Pine Ridge country of northwest Nebraska. Spurred by the energy crisis which increased the demand for fossil fuels, mining operations became profitable. Long Burlington Northern trains moving across the state were a common sight.

Bailey Yard at North Platte is one of the country's largest and most modern freight classification yards. At left is the diesel shop shown on page 208.

Nebraska was the first state to complete its mainline interstate highway system. At a dedication ceremony held on October 19, 1974, five miles west of Sidney, to mark the completion of Interstate 80, a "golden link" (actually a six-inch-wide brass strip embedded in concrete) was uncovered. The cost for the 481 total interstate miles in the state was $400 million. Above, a young couple watch the dedication activities from a nearby hilltop.

This truck center is west of Lincoln, not far from Interstate 80. Major businesses have developed around motor-carrier operations and servicing in Nebraska.

The historic Platte Valley remains the way west—
and east. These twin ribbons of concrete stretching to the horizon are Interstate 80. Flanking
the highway is a chain of lakes, fed by Nebraska's
generous groundwater supply.

By-products of the Panhandle's oil and gas fields are manufactured in Nebraska. Here is the Big Springs gasoline plant of the Kansas-Nebraska Natural Gas Company.

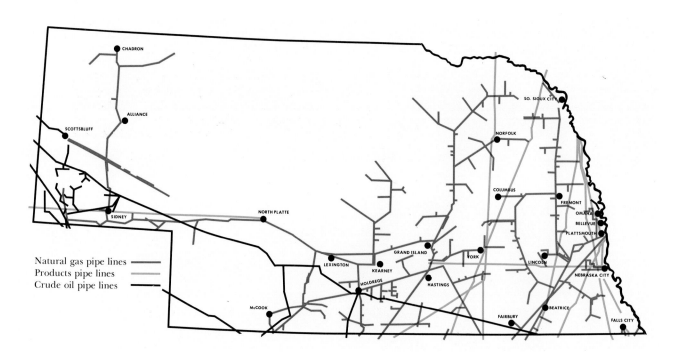

Major underground conduits across Nebraska

Because of its low cost, water transportation of bulk products continues to attract shippers. Here tugs nudge a barge in the Missouri River at Omaha. A deepened channel makes possible shipments far down river to grain terminals and even on to the Gulf.

The nuclear generator at the Cooper Station at Brownville, the largest of its kind between the Mississippi and the West Coast, dwarfs a man standing beside it. Nebraskans in the 1970's were dependent on nuclear generation for much of their power.

Nebraskans, like most American pioneers, raised church spires almost as fast as they raised their first crops. Rural life then as now often centered around the church. Cemeteries sometimes adjoin rural churches where death as a condition of life seems to blend with nature. Shown above is Immanuel Lutheran Church in Seward County. The Cathedral of the Risen Christ, below, shows the influence of modern architectural trends. Located in Lincoln, the cathedral is part of a complex which houses diocesan administrative offices. In the 1960's and '70's most religious institutions were seeking ways to appeal to young people. Though long on tradition, churches found that they were not immune to the forces of change permeating all of society.

Like other former frontier states, Nebraska has known its share of crimes of violence, and the pages of its history are riddled by bullets from handguns and rifles. Often the principals—gunslingers and outlaws—have been romanticized in fiction and popular biography. But the days of western settlement were long past when Lincoln witnessed an outburst of violence unequaled in its recorded history. In 1958 Charles Starkweather and his girl friend Caril Fugate went on a murderous rampage that left twelve persons dead, among them the girl's parents and baby sister. Starkweather died in the electric chair; Fugate was sent to the Women's Reformatory at York to serve a life sentence. Statistically, in the past few years Nebraska has conformed to the rising rate of crime across the nation.

As the air age abolished distance, like their fellow citizens everywhere Nebraskans came to know many national figures as flesh-and-blood people. Very real to them were such leaders as Martin Luther King, John F. Kennedy, and Robert F. Kennedy, each of whom had campaigned or spoken in the state, and the black nationalist Malcolm X, a native Nebraskan. So the assassinations of the 1960's touched Nebraskans directly and personally, affecting them more perhaps than such tragedies ever had before.

Charles Starkweather, shown with Lancaster County Sheriff Merle Karnopp, at the time of his trial.

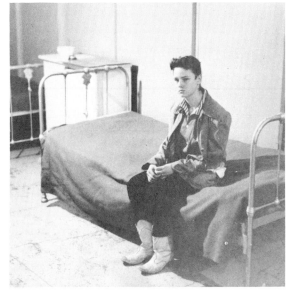

Caril Fugate in jail at Scottsbluff shortly after her capture in Wyoming.

John F. Kennedy spoke at Nebraska Wesleyan University before his nomination as a presidential candidate. There were those who objected to a Catholic politician appearing on the campus of a Methodist institution.

Senator Robert F. Kennedy acccompanied by Astronaut John Glenn, first American to orbit the earth, appeared at Wilber during his campaign for nomination as Democratic presidential candidate in 1968. He won the primary in Nebraska. Senator Kennedy was fatally wounded in Los Angeles on June 5, 1968.

Malcolm X, black nationalist leader who was assassinated in 1965, was born in Omaha. He is shown here while on a visit to his home town.

Dr. Martin Luther King addressed five thousand persons at Pershing Auditorium in Lincoln in 1964. Urging participation in the struggle of black people for equality, Dr. King said citizens should not be like Rip Van Winkle, who slept through the American Revolution. Shown here is a memorial service held in the capitol rotunda following Dr. King's assassination.

Mexican Americans, blacks, and Indians are the chief minority racial groups in Nebraska. For each, in varying situations and locales, the 1960's and '70's were decades of struggle for equal rights. But Indians (many of whom preferred to be called Native Americans) lagged in their battle for freedom, recognition, and economic opportunity. In 1973, just across the Nebraska border north of Rushville, Indians associated with the American Indian Movement took over the village of Wounded Knee (see page 98) as a symbolic center of protest. Many participants were arrested and charged with criminal acts, and some cases were tried in the U.S. District Court in Lincoln. The Nebraska setting recalled the 1879 trial of the Ponca chief Standing Bear. In that historic case, heard in Omaha, Judge Elmer S. Dundy ruled that "an Indian is a person within the meaning of the laws of the United States." The defendants in the Wounded Knee trials moved that their case be dismissed because of lack of federal jurisdiction. The Sioux, they argued, were a sovereign nation by the terms of the Treaty of 1868. In ruling against the motion Judge Warren Urbom noted the "ugly history" of white Americans' relationship with Indians. "Feeling what was wrong does not describe what is right," he said. "Anguish about yesterday does not make alone wise answers for tomorrow. Somehow, all the achings of the soul must coalesce and with the wisdom of the mind develop a single national policy for governmental action." The Indians had lost a legal battle, but they had gained national attention through one of the fullest and most sympathetic hearings ever accorded their cause.

Russell Means

The death of Raymond Yellow Thunder in 1972, following an incident at a Gordon dance hall, stirred Indian anger despite the conviction of several white persons. This episode helped to spark the Indian takeover at Wounded Knee. The two men shown above, Russell Means and Dennis Banks, emerged as leaders of AIM, a militant group involved at Wounded Knee. Their views did not represent those of all Indians, but nevertheless they voiced the frustrations of the race in the 1970's.

Dennis Banks

Many young Nebraskans, primarily students, opposed the war in Southeast Asia. Protests were frequent on college campuses and particularly at the University of Nebraska–Lincoln. Here demonstrators gather on the capitol steps, among them veterans who tossed their medals into a coffin. It was a bitter time with protests coming simultaneously with casualty lists. More than four hundred Nebraskans were killed in the war and many more were wounded.

During the 1960's the women's liberation movement, though poorly defined, gained recognition and gathered momentum, continuing a revolution of sorts. In 1920 women won the right to vote and achieved full citizenship after being political nonpersons. Yet there remained a struggle for economic equality and the acceptance of women as persons of talent, skills, and aspirations. In sum, movement-conscious women insisted that they not be penalized for being either married or single. By the 1970's women held office in many towns and cities, and some were in positions of control or leadership in both business organizations and the professions. Women also were seeking equal status with men in all forms of business transactions, including making contracts and the extension of credit. Women's changing role, and each individual's perception of it, meant adjustments for men, too. But many traditionalists, male and female, were neither ready for nor in agreement with all the concepts of the feminist movement. They felt more comfortable with the customs and relationships of the past.

Nebraskans are politically vocal, so those favoring and opposing the Equal Rights Amendment carried their strong views to their capitol, just as farmers had when they sought a moratorium on mortgage foreclosures (see page 172). This scene is in the rotunda.

Not so many years ago hundreds of one-room schoolhouses dotted the prairies. They had their virtues and their defenders: the pupil-teacher ratio was enviable and a lot of learning was instilled in young heads despite the lack of highly qualified teachers, modern buildings, and adequate equipment. But as time went by improved roads, better transportation, and the pressures to develop broader course offerings resulted in school consolidation. Enlarged school districts and state aid brought upgraded education to thousands of youngsters.

Higher education was moving forward, too. The University of Nebraska developed a systems approach: the chancellor of the two Lincoln campuses and the chancellors of the Medical Center in Omaha and of the Omaha campus (formerly the Municipal University) were responsible to a president and the Board of Regents. There was growth in private colleges; the state college system enrolled many students; and still others availed themselves of the post-secondary vocational training offered in community colleges. As always, financial support was a matter of deep concern to administrators, but handsome new buildings on campuses across the state testified to Nebraskans' commitment to education.

Systems-wide administration of the University
of Nebraska is conducted from Regents Hall,
adjacent to the East Campus in Lincoln.

Broyhill Fountain, north of the Nebraska Union on the City Campus in Lincoln, is a popular and beautiful addition. Oldfather Hall, a classroom and office building seen in the background, is one of several new buildings at UNL.

Milo Bail Student Center Mall is an inviting gathering place on the campus of the University of Nebraska at Omaha.

Nebraska Wesleyan University in Lincoln undertook a major construction program in the 1960's and '70's. Among the additions to its physical plant were the Olin Hall of Science, shown here, a library, fine arts center, campus center, and a classroom-administration building.

Nebraska's private and church-supported colleges are largely concentrated in the eastern third of the state. Here we see the chapel at Hastings College.

This modern library on the Kearney State College campus symbolizes the state's efforts to maintain improved learning facilities in state-supported colleges.

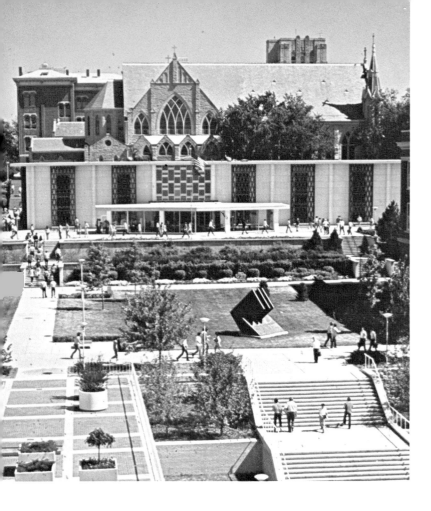

Riggs Plaza on the campus of Creighton University is dominated by the Alumni Memorial Library, but older structures in the background remind visitors that the school has a long history.

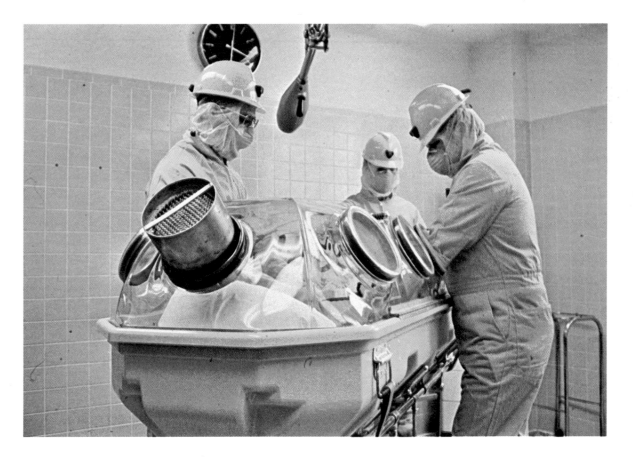

At the University of Nebraska Medical Center in Omaha specialists are trained to handle victims of radiation in the event of accidental exposure. Shown here is a nuclear medicine team at work.

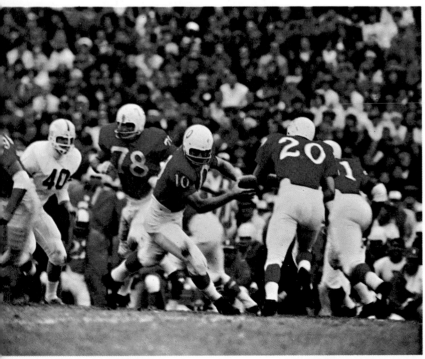

No sporting event—in fact, let's face it, *nothing*—so arouses Nebraskans as a game played by the University of Nebraska football team, known as the Cornhuskers or Big Red. The red you see in the crowd above is not a color distortion. You don't dare set foot in the stadium unless you're wearing something red—hat, tie, belt, shirt, jacket, suspenders, cap. All together now, let's hear it for the team: GO BIG RED!

These students enrolled in electronic engineering are working with equipment on the Milford campus of Southeast Nebraska Technical Community College. Milford was the first state technical school and is now a part of the state system.

In the 1970's Nebraska was evolving an extensive community college system, with some campuses emphasizing technical training and others the liberal arts. One of the latter is Nebraska Western College at Scottsbluff where these students practice for a musical performance.

The Telecommunications Center on the East
Campus at the University of Nebraska–Lincoln
is regarded by many experts as the most advanced
integrated facility in the United States, possibly
in the world. It was designed to meet educational, cultural, governmental, and public-service
needs for all Nebraskans; to accomplish this it
feeds its programming to a network that reaches
all parts of the state (see map on opposite page).

If there was any single development during the past two decades with potential for influencing Nebraskans in a variety of beneficial ways it is the Nebraska Educational Telecommunications Center. Its complex capabilities make it possible to link University of Nebraska classrooms on two campuses, and through SUN (the State University of Nebraska) it brings first- and second-year college courses to off-campus students. Through its various affiliations the Center provides and receives programs from states near and far. For the first time in their history all Nebraskans could hear and see the same program simultaneously. Nebraska launched its now nationally recognized undertaking in this field in modest facilities as recently as 1954. Today it boasts the largest instructional television library in the world.

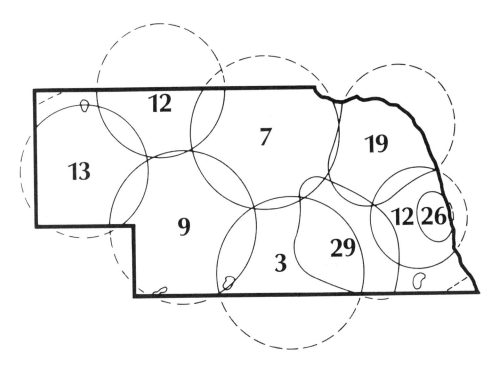

Map of ETV coverage in Nebraska

Applying a variety of techniques to educational and cultural programming, Nebraska Educational Television provides classroom instruction of an order not otherwise possible in many schools.

Emigrants to Nebraska brought with them a heritage of appreciation of literature and the arts. Busy building towns and nurturing crops and cattle they sometimes neglected cultural development, but their sons and daughters went out and made names for themselves as artists, composers, writers, actors, and entertainers. A major cultural renaissance came in the years after World War II. The arts gained significant financial support; community playhouses were established; and audiences flocked to see ballet, hear and view drama and opera performed by touring companies. The Sheldon Memorial Art Gallery in Lincoln and Omaha's Joslyn Art Museum built up important collections; many smaller cities enjoyed traveling art shows and acquired permanent collections housed in colleges and libraries. Painting, photography, and handicrafts became popular hobbies. Moreover, Nebraskans were taking new pride in their history: the past was preserved and recaptured in archives and museums across the state, among them Grand Island's beautiful Stuhr Museum.

The State Fair is a stage where talented people place their most attractive work on display. Shown here is one of many handicraft exhibits.

Variety characterizes Nebraska's farm and gardening activity. This Buffalo County display, showing off the best of the area's produce, salutes the nation's Bicentennial.

Sheldon Memorial Art Gallery on the campus of the University of Nebraska–Lincoln was designed by famed architect Philip Johnson. It houses an outstanding collection of contemporary works.

Through its history Omaha has supported the arts. In the 1890's Willa Cather traveled from Lincoln to view a performance by Sarah Bernhardt. Pictured here is a modern-day production by the Omaha Civic Opera.

Omaha's Joslyn Art Museum houses the noted Bodmer Collection as well as art objects dating from ancient times to the present. The museum is on a hill overlooking the site of the territorial capitol (see page 33).

Concrete evidence of the cultural renaissance was the restoration in 1974 of the opulent Orpheum Theater in downtown Omaha, a widely known center for the performing arts.

In the world of letters, Central City's Wright Morris gained a national reputation for his novels, many set in Nebraska, his photo-text books, and his critical writings. The hundredth anniversary of Willa Cather's birth in 1973 was celebrated by a commemorative postage stamp and a centennial festival at UNL, attended by scholars from many lands. Death came to Mari Sandoz, a daughter of the Sandhills, whose prize-winning biography of her father, *Old Jules,* was the first of the six volumes in her series on the trans-Missouri West which stands as her central achievement. The state also lost its poet laureate, John G. Neihardt, whose books of poetry and prose found a wider, more appreciative audience in his later years than when they had first been published.

John G. Neihardt

Wright Morris

Mari Sandoz

The childhood home of Willa Cather in Red Cloud, restored inside and out by the Willa Cather Pioneer Memorial, was named a National Historic Landmark in 1972.

Shorter work weeks and a growing appreciation of the attractions of their state added new dimensions to the leisure-time activities of an ever-increasing number of Nebraskans. Bicycling, horseback riding, hiking, camping, swimming, water skiing, boating, hunting, exploring historical sites and beauty spots, and just plain loafing in the sun were added to the sports and vacation programs of many families. Promoters of Nebraska publicized its facilities for outdoor recreation as part of "The Good Life." Modern heating and air conditioning combined with year-around comfortable transportation to insulate natives and visitors from the extremes of winter and summer. As Nebraskans recognized and enjoyed the unique features of their environment, they implemented movements to preserve and protect it.

A butte-rimmed valley north of the Wildcat Hills recreation area in western Nebraska.

An autumn landscape in Knox County.

Since the 1930's Nebraskans have been creating lakes. Wherever they are located the waters are soon filled with sailboats, canoes, rowboats, and power craft of all sorts. The scene above shows Lake McConaughy, the state's largest.

Whether these hunters ever got off a shot at waterfowl was almost beside the point. The pleasure of the hunt in quiet waters held its own reward.

Along the Platte Valley and in many other areas of Nebraska, natural beauty spots have been developed for recreation. Station wagons, tents, campers, trailers, and boats are now standard equipment for many families.

The strange shapes of the land in the northwestern Nebraska Badlands

Lightning display during a summer storm near Niobrara

Weather is more than a prime topic of conversation in Nebraska; it's an obsession. There is elemental violence here—tornadoes, hail, freezing rain, cloudbursts, extreme heat and extreme cold. Conversely, we have soft snows, gentle rains, and many sunny days.

In the series of photographs at the left, a tornado drops out of the summer sky and almost erases the small village of Primrose (bottom). On May 6, 1975, tornadoes ravaged parts of Omaha, leaving several persons dead and destroying millions of dollars worth of property. It was perhaps the most destructive storm in the state's history, but early warnings saved lives.

Typically the Nebraska sky in summer is brilliantly blue and splashed with immense billowing white clouds floating lazily eastward, as in the Sandhills scene above. In the Seward County farmstead scene below, the land lies locked in winter.

Omaha, Nebraska's largest city, had a population of more than 346,000 according to the 1970 census, and ranked forty-first among U.S. cities. About one-third of the state's population is concentrated in the Omaha metropolitan area, embracing Douglas, Sarpy, and Washington counties. The area elects fifteen of the forty-nine senators in Nebraska's one-house legislature, a politically significant fact illustrating the one-man, one-vote principle. Urban senators hold a strong hand in the state that reaches almost five hundred miles westward from the Missouri River to the Wyoming border. Omaha is a major transportation and industrial complex; among the tourist attractions are Boys Town and Henry Doorly Zoo. Just south of Omaha, in Bellevue, is the headquarters of the Strategic Air Command. Its underground control center (left) is in communication with installations and aircraft around the world.

Lincoln, the second largest city, is the site of Nebraska's magnificent state capitol, considered one of the architectural wonders of the world (left). Two denominational colleges and universities are located there, as well as the University of Nebraska's Lincoln and East Campuses. The beautiful Sheldon Memorial Art Gallery and the Nebraska State Museum, featuring the Mueller Planetarium and Elephant Hall, are located on the downtown campus. Adjacent to it is the Nebraska State Historical Society, with its fine museum and archives. While Lincoln has been known as a retail and wholesale trading center and the home of several large insurance companies, in recent years it has been actively seeking industry. Lincoln's skyline is seen below from Oak Creek Lake with an autumn moon illuminating the sky.